ADAM FERNER

THINK DIFFERENTLY

OPEN YOUR MIND. PHILOSOPHY FOR MODERN LIFE.

Brimming with creative inspiration, how-to projects and useful information to enrich your everyday life, Quarto Knows is a favourite destination for those pursuing their interests and passions. Visit our site and dig deeper with our books into your area of interest: Quarto Creates, Quarto Cooks, Quarto Homes, Quarto Lives, Quarto Drives, Quarto Explores, Quarto Gifts, or Quarto Kids.

First published in 2018 by Aurum Press
an imprint of The Quarto Group
The Old Brewery, 6 Blundell Street
London N7 9BH
United Kingdom

www.QuartoKnows.com

A catalogue record for this book is available from the British Library.

ISBN 978 1 78131 717 4
Ebook ISBN 978 1 78131 777 8

10 9 8 7 6 5 4 3 2 1
2022 2021 2020 2019 2018

Designed and illustrated by Stuart Tolley of Transmission Design

Printed in China by 1010 Printing International Limited

For Celia and Robin

CONTENTS

INTRODUCTION   08

HOW TO USE THIS BOOK   10

01 PEOPLE SKILLS

01 How to Argue   18
02 Telling the Truth   22
03 Respect   28
04 The Limits of Loyalty   32

→   Toolkit 01—04   36
✚   Further Learning   38

02 LIFESTYLE

05 Marriage   44
06 Making Babies   48
07 Eating Meat   54
08 Shopping   58

→   Toolkit 05—08   62
✚   Further Learning   64

03 SELF-HELP

09	Staying Alive	70
10	The Real Me	74
11	Dealing with Death	80
12	Death and Taxes	84
→	Toolkit 09—12	88
+	Further Learning	90

04 SOCIETY

13	Group Mentality	96
14	Club Rules	100
15	Making Amends	106
16	Moral Rubbish	110
→	Toolkit 13—16	114
+	Further Learning	116

05 RECREATION

17	Horror Films	122
18	Fine Dining	126
19	Creative Genius	132
20	Virtual life	136
→	Toolkit 17—20	140
+	Further Learning	142
	Epilogue	144

INTRODUCTION

Let's be honest: philosophy isn't very good at giving us answers. For literally thousands of years, philosophers have been asking the same old questions without producing any real solutions. Do we have free will? Is there an immortal soul? Some say 'kind of', some say 'probably not', but most people just shrug their shoulders.

This isn't a failing of philosophy, however. Some questions don't have hard and fast answers – and often the 'philosophical shrug' is the only appropriate response to the multiple confusions that emerge from our hodgepodge of existence. Philosophy isn't a matter of drawing up a list of what's true and what's not. It's about becoming puzzled *in a useful way*. It's about seeing complexity and embracing it. That's the aim of this book too – to help you become more puzzled,

confused and fascinated by the world we inhabit, and the people we share it with.

There are five chapters in all, each split into four lessons. The first, 'People Skills', goes through various theories and thoughts about our personal encounters with other people. Is it ever okay to lie? Why do we argue? What does it mean to respect your parents? Chapter 2, 'Lifestyle', looks at our lifestyle choices and how we make them. Do you want to get married and have babies? How come? If you're a vegetarian, should you be a vegan? Is nut-cheese evil? The third chapter is called 'Self-Help' and focuses on the self. Your self, my self – what are these mysterious 'self' things? What happens to them when you die? Are they the product of a particular political perspective? (Watch out, this chapter might

'There is but one coward on earth,
and that is the coward that dare
not know.'
W.E.B. Du Bois

be uncomfortable reading for those prone to existential angst.) 'Society' is the theme for Chapter 4. It examines the way we split ourselves into groups along supposedly 'natural' lines, and the invisible ideological forces that shape the ways we think. The fifth and final chapter, 'Recreation', covers hobbies and pastimes from horror films to computer games. Is it ever okay to enjoy fictional representations of violence? Is creativity learned or innate? And is Marmite objectively disgusting?

Each of these chapters uses work in contemporary epistemology, metaphysics, aesthetics and politics to examine *everyday* issues – because philosophy shouldn't just be a matter of obscure logical problems and esoteric musings. It should be about our lives and about how we live them.

HOW TO USE THIS BOOK

This book is organised into five parts and 20 key lessons covering the most current and topical debates of philosophy today.

Each lesson introduces you to an important concept,

and explains how you can apply what you've learned to everyday life.

As you go through the book, TOOLKITS help you keep track of what you've learned so far.

Specially curated FURTHER LEARNING notes give you a nudge in the right direction for those things that most captured your imagination.

BUILD + BECOME

At BUILD+BECOME we believe in building knowledge that helps you navigate your world. So, dip in, take it step-by-step, or digest it all in one go – however you choose to read this book, enjoy and get thinking.

LIKE THE SU
A DONUT, P
COVERS AB
EVERYTHING

GAR FROM
HILOSOPHY
SOLUTELY

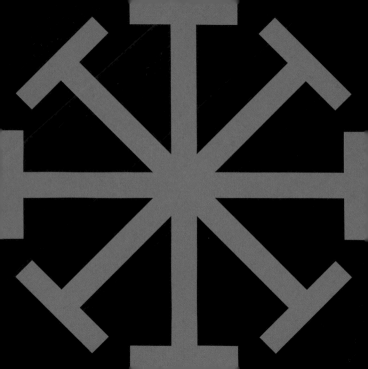

PEOPLE SKILLS

LESSONS

01 HOW TO ARGUE
Arguments are essential for generating new ideas. So is it weird to think they're oppositional?

02 TELLING THE TRUTH
Is it ever okay to lie? Can a lie be a victimless act? Immanuel Kant says 'no' – should we trust him?

03 RESPECT
We respect different things; laws, nature and people. Do we respect them in the same way?

04 THE LIMITS OF LOYALTY
It seems obvious that loyalty is a virtue and disloyalty is a failing. But just because something's obvious doesn't make it true.

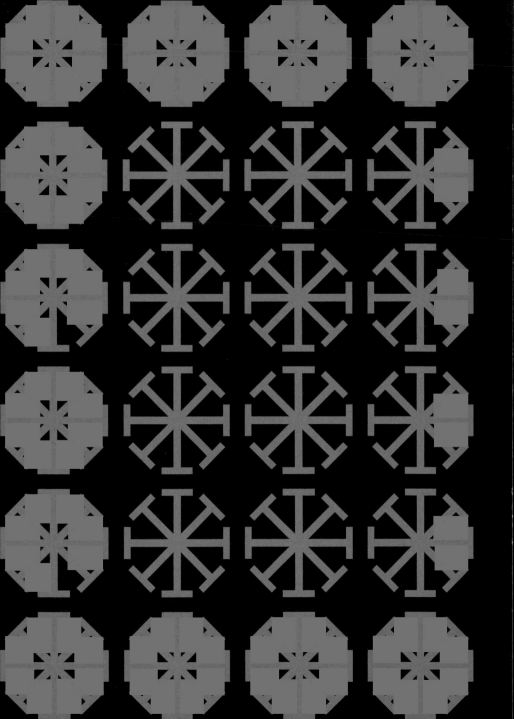

'Morally as well as physically, there is only one world, and we all have to live in it.'
Mary Midgley

In this chapter we're going to look at what folk in management would call 'people skills': *interpersonal relationships*. How do we interact with others? And, importantly, can philosophy help us see better ways of doing so? The Lessons focus on ethical behaviours we exhibit – and sometimes fail to exhibit – in our day-to-day dealings with other people. Whether at home or at work, out shopping or on the bus, the way we interact with other human beings is unendingly fascinating. Even the most humdrum encounter can benefit from philosophical investigation.

Say you're arguing with your buddy over what to have for dinner – pizza or curry? *How* are you arguing? And *why*? Are you open to having your mind changed?

What about if you want to call in sick – is it bad to lie to your boss? Even if they don't find out, what happens when you corrupt the capital T: Truth?

And think of all the times you're told to 'respect your parents'. Is this just parental propaganda? In order to know whether it's sound advice, we have to work out what 'respect' is, and when and whether it's appropriate.

Loyalty is another issue. When our friends criticize us to other people, we think they're being 'disloyal'. We rarely stop to wonder whether what they've said is justified. Maybe disloyalty isn't such a bad thing ...

In each situation, philosophical examination can help us understand what's going on, and whether it might be ethical or unethical, effective or ineffective. Each of the lessons can be read independently of the others, although there are not insignificant links between them. At the end of the chapter, we'll look at the lessons we've learned and start building our philosophical toolkit.

HOW TO ARGUE

Argument is a blood sport – that's how many of us see it at any rate. We talk about engaging in a 'battle of wits', delivering 'killer blows' or seeing 'fatal flaws' in other people's positions. When you describe the 'cut and thrust' of debate, you're describing people stabbing each other – which is, it must be said, pretty grisly stuff.

Of course, these are metaphors. Things might get heated, but you tend not to literally shoot down your opponent in the middle of a conversation. In fact, a lot of the time arguments are amicable; it's not uncommon to actively enjoy the parry and riposte element, in the same way you might enjoy a game of ping-pong. And like competitive sports, we think of arguments as things we can win or lose. If you've prepared your defences well and speak with sufficient dexterity, you can vanquish your adversary. You can dazzle them with rhetoric, undermine their premises or simply shout them down. It doesn't much matter how you do it – the aim, we think, is to triumph.

But is this central to what an argument is?

The answer to this question depends, predictably, on the context in which the argument is taking place. If you're in a debating squad preparing for a semi-final, it's very much expected that there will be adversaries and, ultimately, a victor. Points are scored. There are judges to adjudicate. You might, if you're lucky, even win a prize at the end.

Sadly, not all arguments work like this – most of the time we don't get prizes. More importantly, the arguments we engage with in our daily lives are rarely so cut and dried or as static as they are in competitions.

Consider the structure of arguments. There are 'premises' – for example, the claims that 'all humans are mortal' and 'Rebecca is a human'. And there's a 'conclusion' that's supposed to follow from the premises, such as 'Rebecca is mortal'. In a competitive debate, you're assigned a pre-established conclusion, like 'Money is evil', and you're supposed to defend it without compromise while undermining your adversary (who holds the opposite view). There are various ways to argue that money is evil, and the debaters can deploy different premises, but ultimately they can't relinquish their conclusion. They have to hold their position. If they don't, we can't say whether the debate has been won or lost.

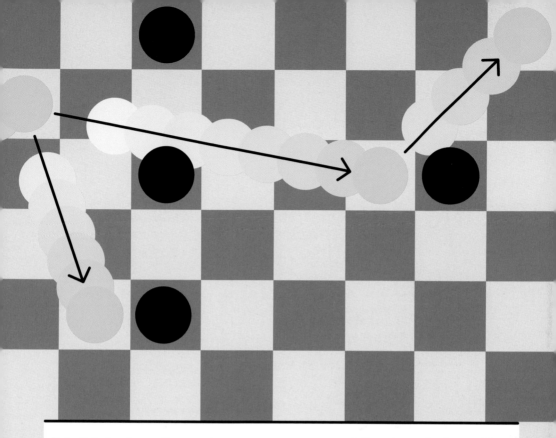

But what about an ordinary exchange, one you might have in the office? Jim from accounts keeps taking your pens – the scoundrel. You complain, telling him how annoying it is. Jim, being Jim, replies that pens are a small price to pay for having the best seat in the office (which admittedly you do). That's annoying, he says, if anything is. A seat right next to the water fountain. And the fan. And the snacks.

Sure, you might try and win this argument. You were assigned your seat, you may say. He, however, is *wilfully* nabbing pens. He's in the wrong. The argument could carry on, with both of you listing your petty grievances and the reasons you're right. And maybe you will win. Perhaps, with your rhetorical

prowess and disarming verbosity, you'll succeed in irritating poor Jim right out of the room. But will your winning have *solved* anything? Will that even constitute winning? In all likelihood, Jim will continue to take your pens and resent you for sitting where you sit. This is a context in which the winning or losing element drops away, and another feature of arguments comes to the fore.

Arguments can be used to *solve* things. Imagine if, instead of trying to beat Jim, you try to recognize the truth of his position and adjust your own position accordingly. Perhaps a compromise can be reached? Perhaps the water fountain could be moved? Perhaps (dare I say it) some more snacks could be bought?

WINNING FROM SOLVING

So here are two different forms of argument. On the one hand, an argument can be a kind of game, to be won or lost. On the other, an argument can be a way of problem-solving or exploring ideas. There are no winners *per se*, and participants don't lose anything if they relinquish their original position.

Take a moment to think about how you normally argue. Do you argue to win? This is how a lot of people – from philosophers to lawyers and politicians – are trained. And it's significant that this approach puts up tangible obstacles to understanding. The game requires you to defend your starting point, even in the face of good evidence to relinquish it. In some sense, this leads to what we might call 'epistemic losses', a setback in what you know. Even on its own terms, winning isn't quite what it's cracked up to be. Phyllis Rooney, in her paper 'Philosophy, Adversarial Argumentation, and Embattled Reason' (2010), puts this point well:

'I lose the argument and you win ... But surely I am the one who has made the epistemic gain, however small. I have replaced a probably false belief with a probably true one, and you have made no such gain...'

When you use argument as a form of problem-solving, everybody ends up better off. The focus isn't on defending a position at whatever cost – it's on gaining understanding, hopefully even access to truth. Objections can still be raised and rebutted, but in a spirit of collaboration and mutual respect (as we'll see in Lesson 3).

This distinction isn't simply academic. It's crucial. One kind of argument is aggressive and can impede understanding. The other can generate solutions and agreement. A competitive argument is static, but a collaborative argument is dynamic.

The next time you see an argument – whether a family dispute or a political debate – have a think about who's winning and who's losing. Who's *trying* to win? And might the argument be more productive if people stopped point-scoring and began to collaborate?

OPEN DISCUSSION

FIXED POSITION

TELLING THE TRUTH

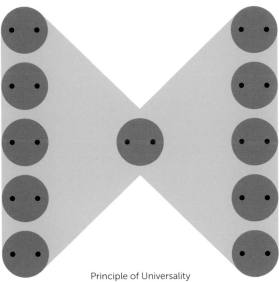

Principle of Universality

Immanuel Kant was nothing if not ambitious; in his book *Groundwork of the Metaphysics of Morals* (1785), he aimed to map out the structure of what he saw to be an objective moral reality. He claimed that there are incontrovertible moral facts – some acts are just always going to be wrong (murder most foul). There's no wishy-washy, hand-waving 'matter of opinion'. Moral truths do not depend on your perspective; they're facts, wherever you're standing.

It was this objective moral reality that he took himself to be tapping into with his concept of the 'categorical imperative'. It's a multifaceted notion of what it is, categorically, *imperative* that people do if they are to be moral. It's one concept, a single, formal moral law, but it has different formulations. For the sake of

present purposes, we can focus on the first two. To begin with, we've got the Principle of Universality, which states:

'Act only according to that maxim whereby you can at the same time will that it should become a universal law.'

Kant isn't really known for snappy writing – but in essence, this is a version of the 'do unto others' idea that you find in most religions. When you act in a certain way, you should consider whether it would be okay if everyone acted in that way. Say you decide to start filching other people's chocolates – would it be okay if everybody did that? How would we get by if everyone was always filching everyone else's chocolates (or money, or lives)?

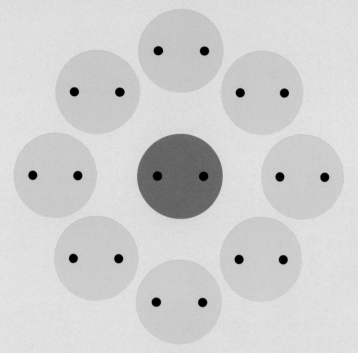

Principle of Humanity

The second formulation is known as the Principle of Humanity and states, roughly, that you should always treat others as 'ends in themselves' rather than as means to some end of your own. When dealing with friends and strangers, you have always to bear in mind that they've got their own lives, with their own hopes and dreams (and they must recognize that you have all of these things too). At the centre of Kant's ethical system is the thought that we must respect the dignity and equality of human beings. If we fail to do so, if we *use* other people, we commit a moral violation.

Imagine, for instance, that you want to impress your boss by making your work-mate look like an idiot. Even if you don't hold a particular grudge against Gilbert, you'd be failing to acknowledge his humanity; you'd be treating him as a stepping stone, not a person.

Kant's moral system has its drawbacks. For one thing, as Lewis R. Gordon has pointed out (and we'll see in Lesson 13), the man was a horrible racist – so his claims about the importance of universal respect for human beings seem hypocritical at best. For another thing, his picture is hugely formalistic. In claiming that there's an objective moral reality, he paints our ethical world in black and white with no shades of grey.

However, despite these failings, his categorial imperitive has been hugely influential – not least because it aspires to flesh out a moral system without appear to theology. His *Groundwork* is an exercise in reason alone – so it speaks equally, he contends, to all human beings.

AIMING FOR TRUTH

There are a whole host of lies you can tell. You've got your little white lies and your whoppers, and typically we think some are worse than others. If you told me you don't like asparagus, but secretly you do, I wouldn't mind too much. If you told me you haven't murdered anyone when actually you have – well, that's another matter. Some lies seem to be more serious than others.

Kant, however, thinks all lies are equally bad – because lying, as an act, violates the second formulation of the categorical imperative, *The Principle of Humanity*. For Kant, human dignity and equality are of the utmost importance. We should never treat humans, he says, as anything less than what they are – free, rational agents with unique and self-governable lives. When you lie to a human, you've stopped treating them in this way because you've deprived them of the ability to assess a situation rationally and to respond to it freely.

Consider a story (100% fictional). I'm short of cash and want to go to the cinema. I ask you to lend me £20 – and I tell you I need it to pay my rent (lie) because I think you're less likely to lend it to me if you think I'm just going to fritter it away on pick n' mix. Being the generous soul you are, you lend me the cash and I go and glut myself on sweeties and my third viewing of some trashy Hollywood blockbuster.

In this scenario, I've deceived you to further my own end. I've robbed you of the ability to assess the situation rationally (by depriving you of salient facts) and so I've undermined your ability to choose freely to give me the money. I'm treating you as a means to an end rather than an end in yourself, like a cash-machine rather than a person.

Of course, there are trickier cases. Take the story of the axe-wielding maniac, often trotted out in the philosophical literature. If he asks you where your loved ones are, should you lie to save their lives? In a less melodramatic vein, consider a situation where a lie might save a friend's feelings from getting hurt. Should you ever promise that 'everything will be all right', without knowing that it will?

Kant's response to these kinds of cases is famously hard-line. He says you should never lie. Never ever. It's not surprising he's been accused of adopting a rather unsubtle approach to moral theory. At the same time, we can see this as another example of a certain kind of ambitiousness. He thinks we should never lie – but that doesn't mean we should let the axe-wielding maniac kill our loved ones. We should create a world where such maniacs either don't exist or don't get to ask us questions. And, similarly, we should nurture our friends and our friendships so that we don't have to lie in order to reassure them. All in all, that doesn't sound like a terrible idea.

IF LOYALTY'
MAYBE DISL
BE A VIRTUE

S A VIRTUE,
OYALTY CAN
TOO?

RESPECT

Respect each other. That seems like a fairly good rule of thumb for our everyday interactions. 'Love each other' isn't always workable, since love isn't necessarily the kind of thing you can turn on or off. And 'tolerate each other' isn't much better; you tolerate or ignore bad smells, and treating people like bad smells is a terrible rule of thumb – it doesn't foster understanding or lead to harmonious living.

But is everyone worthy of respect? What about racists? Homophobes and sexists? Should we respect those who spout prejudice? If you find yourself faced with a bigot spewing dangerous hate speech, I'm guessing you're going to find it hard to 'respect' them. So maybe we think there are people who aren't worthy of respect?

Maybe ... but let's think a little harder about the issue.

Unless you lead an unbelievably sheltered life, it's easy to find yourself confronted by people whose views you fundamentally disagree with. Arguments often result. And sometimes these arguments escalate because, in spite of your best efforts, it appears impossible to find common ground. There's no compromise. You don't just disagree with them, you think their views are dangerous and should be called out as such. They think, for example, that women are genetically configured to do housework – you think this is an abhorrent and ridiculous thing to say.

How does all this square with the seemingly sensible claim that we should 'respect each other'?

Well, what is respect exactly? We respect different things in different ways. We respect nature (like the sea and its terrifying power), and concepts (like the speed limit and the law). 'Respect' can mean 'don't underestimate'; don't underestimate the ocean and its ability to pulverize your boat. It can be a call to recognize the importance of something, and the consequences if you fail to do so. The speed limit is an important part of traffic regulations – if you don't respect it, bad things happen.

And of course, we respect people too – also in a variety of ways. If you say, 'I respect Martin Luther King Jr', that would likely mean you admire him. But not everyone is so admirable. The suggestion above that we should 'respect each other' uses 'respect' in a slightly different sense. This usage is closer to what we were talking about in Lesson 2; when we respect people, we treat them as ends in themselves. We treat them as unique entities that have value in and of themselves. The political philosopher Kwame Anthony Appiah connects respect with the notion of human dignity. We're all humans, he says, irrespective of our political views – and we need to recognize this when we're interacting with one another. It's not what we *say* that garners respect, in this sense, but what we *are*.

I RESPECTFULLY DISAGREE

Let's return to the bigot. Undignified as they may seem, they're still human and possessors of human dignity. In fact, we should probably stop calling them a 'bigot'. It's not helpful. Despite all the hateful things they say, they're worthy of our respect (if not our admiration).

What does this mean in practical terms? What should we do when faced with people who say atrocious things? Shout? Jeer? Throw rotten fruit? No, says Appiah. If you respect them in this philosophical sense, then you'll talk to them about their ideas.

It is, Appiah says in his essay 'Relativism and Cross-Cultural Understanding' (2010),

'better to treat one another's moral beliefs as responsive to reasons, because to treat a person's moral views as bare facts about them, ungrounded in reasons, is to treat them with disrespect.' If you respect someone, this involves seeing them as human, as beings with a capacity for thought and self-determination, as responsive to reasons. They're more than just by-products of a cultural milieu. They're people who can assess facts and analyze them, and come to judgments for themselves.

Imagine your grandmother says that being gay is 'wicked'. Now, you love your grandmother but it's a horrible thing to hear.

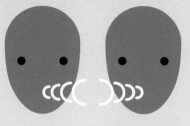

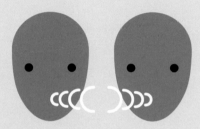

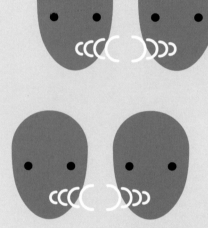

So what do you do? Well, on the one hand you could just shrug – 'She's a product of her time', you tell your friends, 'She doesn't know any better'. That, thinks Appiah, would be to treat your grandmother with disrespect. Of course, like anyone, there are deep-seated, culturally located reasons why she says the things she does. But your grandmother is human too. She has the capacity to think and reason, and form decisions for herself. If you respect her, and see her as a possessor of human dignity, you'll talk to her and explain, as well as you can, why it's hurtful and wrong to say that being gay is wicked. Her moral views are not bare facts about her.

When you revert to calling someone an idiot or close down a discussion, you're being disrespectful insofar as you're seeing your interlocutor as someone who can't be reasoned with. It might be that, in the end, the obstacles are too great and neither of you can effectively communicate your rationale for the beliefs. Appiah's point, however, is that it's crucial to give the person the benefit of the doubt and to expect the same in return. You have to make yourself responsive to reasons, and so should whoever you're talking to. It's respect in *this* sense that one should aim for in arguments.

THE LIMITS OF LOYALTY

When was the last time you felt betrayed? Have a good think ... got it? It's a horrible feeling, isn't it? Really gut-churning. It's tremendously upsetting to discover someone you trusted has abused that trust. The connection you thought you had has been severed, perhaps irrevocably, and the time, effort and love that's gone into a relationship has all gone to waste.

Betrayal comes in many forms. You can betray your partner by hooking up with others; you can betray your country by selling its secrets; you can betray your friends by talking dirt about them behind their backs. You can betray yourself too, by failing to live up to the principles you tell yourself to abide by.

The harmful effects of these betrayals can be far-reaching. If you betray your partner, you imperil your relationship. You also imperil future relationships – if you've cheated on someone you love, who's to say you won't do so again? You damage your status as a 'trustworthy' individual. Betrayal can be seen as an indication of weakness and inconstancy.

It's because of these harms that we have so many damning terms for betrayers: fair-weather friends, turncoats, traitors, snitches, sneaks, weasels, rats ... And it's because of these harms that we often figure loyalty is a good thing.

The 19th-century American philosopher Josiah Royce wrote in his book, *The Philosophy of Loyalty* (1908), that loyalty is 'the willing and practical and thorough-going devotion of a person to a cause'. We can be loyal to ideals and institutions. More recently, the moral philosopher, Marcia Brown, has pointed out that we more typically take 'loyalty' to refer to a relationship between *persons*. You can be loyal to your partner if, despite being attracted to someone else, you nevertheless remain faithful. You can be loyal to your friend if, despite pressure to sell them out, you keep schtum. We tend to prize these kinds of actions and typically label loyalty as 'a virtue'.

Loyalty offers security. If you're the nervous type, your partner's loyalty will offer considerable comfort. And loyalty is good for both you and the recipient. If you're loyal to something (a football club, for example), your relationship to that thing is enhanced. You identify with the institution or person or principle that you're loyal to. If I'm loyal to my family, and put the needs of my family before my own, it's because, in a way, I see my own needs as inextricably tied up with theirs.

Loyalty, then, seems to be a good thing. But seeming is different from being. Is loyalty so certain a virtue?

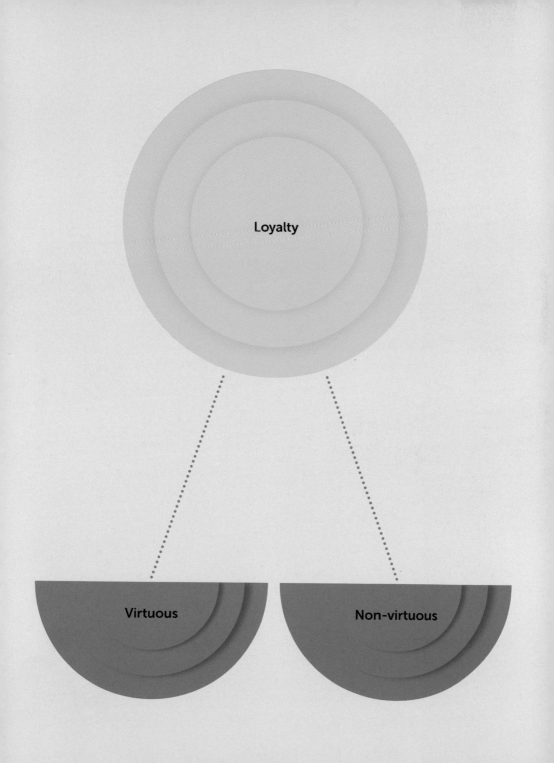

Loyalty

Virtuous

Non-virtuous

LOYALTY

DISLOYALTY

THE VALUES OF DISLOYALTY

'Loyalty confines you to accepted opinions; loyalty forbids you to comprehend sympathetically your dissident fellows...' *Graham Greene*

'The first thing I want to teach is disloyalty till they get used to disusing that word loyalty as representing a virtue. This will beget independence...' *Mark Twain*

There are, as these quotations attest, a few folk who are slightly more circumspect about the so-called virtue of loyalty. The general thought, articulated by the novelists Twain and Greene, is that loyalty is restrictive. It undermines your independence. It's a form of control. The examples discussed above show us its positive effects, but there are plenty of cases where it can have slightly more dubious results.

Consider Akosua. She has been working hard at her job for a couple of years and has swiftly risen to managerial level. Perhaps she has been helped in some minimal way by one of the partners in the firm: a kindly old soul called John. One day Akosua discovers that John has been paying for fancy dinners with the company credit card. It's wrong, and she knows it. So should she report him? The Johns of this world typically rely on a 'sense of loyalty' to keep people less powerful than themselves quiet. Would disloyalty in this situation really be a bad thing?

It's easy to imagine even more troubling cases where people in power use loyalty to silence their employees and co-workers.

As Marcia Baron points out in *The Moral Status of Loyalty* (1984), there are numerous instances of disloyalty having beneficial effects and undermining objectionable institutions. Remember, it's the concept of loyalty – to one's queen, or lord – which supported the hugely unequal feudal society. And it's disloyalty, or 'whistle blowing', that means that otherwise well-protected industries that benefit from, for example, slave labour, can be brought to justice. Disloyalty to presidents, queens and company bosses can bring to light hidden abuses of power.

Loyalty, says Baron, can stand as an obstacle to justice. It's a dissuasive force that encourages you to leave certain things unquestioned. This thoroughgoing commitment to a person or cause overrides your ability to critique the objects of your loyalty effectively. The consequences of such loyalty can be horrendous. Take, for example, the German soldiers who were unthinkingly loyal to the Third Reich, or the British citizens who gave unswerving loyalty to the empire and its exploitative colonial activities.

Sure, loyalty can prevent you from doing bad things. It can stop you from cheating on your partner. But loyalty also protects others when they do bad things. It allows businesses to continue in their dodgy dealings, and leaves individuals open to exploitation. The effects of loyalty can be both positive and negative – and, interestingly, the same is true for disloyalty. So if loyalty's a virtue, maybe disloyalty can be one too?

TOOLKIT

01

Much of the time we argue *competitively* – as though we can win or lose – but there are distinct advantages to arguing *collaboratively*. Two heads are better than one.

Thinking point Do you think more carefully if you're arguing to win?

02

When you lie to someone you take away their ability to reason – so, according to Kant, you should always tell the truth (even when faced with an axe-wielding criminal).

Thinking point If reason is what matters, is it okay to lie to someone with a severe mental impairment?

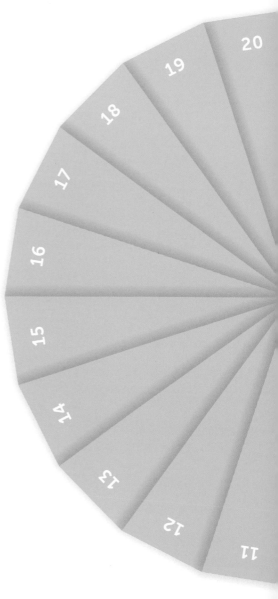

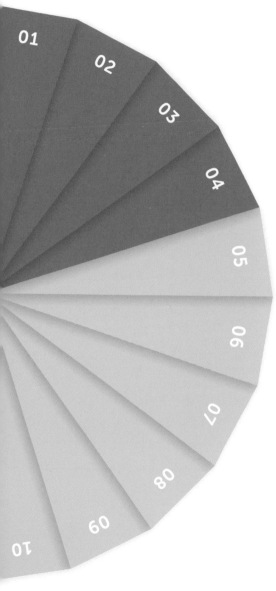

01
02
03
04
05
06
07
08
09
10

03

Respect can mean either *admiration* or *acknowledgement of human dignity*. The latter means seeing someone as responsive to reasons.
Thinking point When was the last time a bigot changed your mind?

04

Loyalty can enhance your relationships with other people (and football clubs), but sometimes disloyalty can be very valuable in exposing exploitative systems.
Thinking point Are there ever cases where loyalty is more important than justice?

FURTHER LEARNING

READ

Two Kinds of Respect
Stephen Darwall, *Ethics* (1977)

Loving Your Enemies
Martin Luther King Jr, (1957)
www.kingencyclopedia.stanford.edu/
encyclopedia/documentsentry/doc_loving_
your_enemies.1.html

Relativism, Persons, and Practices
Amelie Rorty, in *Relativism: A Contemporary Anthology* (Colombia University Press, 2010)

LISTEN

'Political Distrust' (Episode 13), The UnMute Podcast
Presented by Myisha Cherry with Meena Krishnamurthy. You should listen to the UnMute Podcast right now! It's full to bursting with fascinating discussions – all hosted by the excellent Myisha Cherry.

WATCH

Beau Travail
Directed by Claire Denis, this stunning and disturbing film about life in the French Foreign Legion demonstrates some of the complex ways in which lies, respect and loyalty intersect.

Fargo
A strange and blackly comic television series, FX's *Fargo* examines the lies and betrayals that result after an insurance salesman, Lester Nygaard, commits murder.

Wi-Phi
'Wireless Philosophy' is a fantastic, free online resource of short videos covering a range of political and philosophical topics

VISIT

How the Light Gets In
The annual Hay-On-Wye philosophy and music festival brings together philosophers, politicians, novelists and musicians to discuss anything from angst to Zeno's paradoxes. Definitely worth popping along.

LIFESTYLE

LESSONS

05 MARRIAGE
What better way to celebrate your love than by getting married?
Well, maybe by not getting married.

06 MAKING BABIES
People seem to like making babies — but is there a moral
imperative to adopt or foster *pre-existing* children?

07 EATING MEAT
Vegetarianism looks like an ethical response to the horrors of
the meat industry, but isn't veganism better? How do we meet
all these moral concerns?

08 SHOPPING
'Commodity fetishism' isn't a sex thing — it's a powerful
concept for explaining our attitudes to all the junk that we're
tempted to buy.

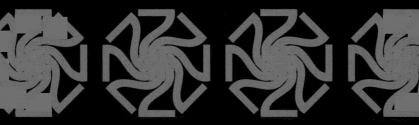

'Life is more than earning a living, and if you're not in the habit of thinking about it, you can end up middle-aged or even older and shocked to realize that your life seems empty.'
Martha C. Nussbaum

Every so often we're faced with big life decisions: should I get married? Should I have a baby? Should I eat meat? And the smaller ones: should I buy that brand-new pair of sneakers even though my old ones are barely worn? Our answers to these questions constitute our style of living – or, more pithily, our 'lifestyle'. This is the focus of the present chapter.

Much of the time, if we're thinking about marriage or making babies, the question is not whether but when. Should I marry this person now? Am I at a stage in my life when I can look after a bawling infant? The aim in this chapter is to look at the 'whether' questions: whether I should get married at all; whether I should have a baby (and if so, how?) We're also going to look at more routine activities. Most people eat meat and go shopping on a daily basis; what are the ethical quandaries these situations provoke? If we don't eat meat, what *can* we eat? And are 'commodities' really as straightforward as they first appear?

One thing that will become clear over the following pages is that all these questions are interlinked. Being a vegetarian isn't just about what food you put in your mouth; it's about what clothes you buy and who you vote for. Likewise, the decision to have a baby may have just as many environmental consequences as factory farming. This thought, that there are no discrete areas of ethical concern, is found in the work of philosophers from Aristotle to Patricia Hill Collins. It's one to keep in mind as we go through the following lessons.

MARRIAGE

There are countless reasons to get married. You and your partner are head-over-heels in love. You want to announce your commitment to each other by enacting one of the oldest love rituals in human history. You also like tax breaks – just one of the many practical benefits enjoyed by married couples. Other benefits include improved social standing and certain legal rights (relating to inheritances and hospital visits). Visas are another reason to get married. And if those weren't enough, think of the snazzy dresses and blowout parties.

Collectively these reasons might seem persuasive, but what about individually? Imagine you ask a bride-to-be why she's getting married and she answers, 'Because of the tax-breaks.' Her husband-in-waiting adds: 'And my visa.' Huh? Neither response seems to be in 'the spirit' of marriage – this ancient institution is being seen as a way of attaining practical benefits. If you ask someone why they're eating an apple and they say, 'Because it's low in calories,' they might as well eat a rice-cake. If they say 'Because I *love* the appley taste!' you can only say, 'Fair enough'.

Philosophers often separate things into *intrinsic* goods, i.e. ones that are essential to an activity, and *extrinsic* goods, which are not. Tax breaks, visas, parties, rings and party rings are *extrinsic* goods – and while they might constitute reasons to get married, they might also constitute reasons to, for example, enter into a civil partnership. They're 'add-ons'.

The Cambridge philosopher Clare Chambers suggests that marriage is an institution that people enter into largely because of the meanings it represents. Add-ons aside, there's something about marriage itself that's seen to be valuable. In her essay, 'The Marriage-Free State' (2003), she writes:

'Couples may marry so as to obtain various practical benefits, but a key aspect of most marriages is the statement the couples make about their relationship. For the marrying couple and for society in general, the symbolic significance of marriage is at least as important as its practical aspects ... This being the case, it is impossible to escape the history of the institution. Its status as a tradition ties its current meaning to its past.'

So some folk think marriage is valuable in and of itself – because of what it means – and, as Chambers indicates, its meaning is a function of the historical, cultural processes that produced the tradition. The wedding ceremony is one example of the way in which marriage can provide a rich vocabulary – of symbolic gestures and rites – with which a couple can declare their mutual love and commitment, in front of society and (depending on their religious inclinations) in front of God. These things are intrinsic to the ancient tradition.

That all seems fine ... until we start looking at this history more closely. What are we really buying into when we say 'I do'?

BUILDING NEW TRADITIONS

In her essay, Clare Chambers describes marriage's troubling past. It figures, unfortunately, as an institution that has given rise to numerous human rights violations – most obviously, against women. Philosophers and historians, from Simone de Beauvoir to Ralph Wedgewood, have described how, from its earliest days, marriage has construed women as commodities to be exchanged. Brides are seen as bargaining chips, used to secure advantageous links between families – and of course, for the production of heirs.

We may, of course, think the institution no longer functions in this way. Same-sex marriage is now widely, if not universally, recognized. Women can even keep their names if they like! Sure, the response goes, the whole thing used to be rather suspect, but institutions can *change*. Once upon a time, Western democracy denied women the right to vote. It's different now. Can't the same be true for marriage?

Chamber's central point is that most people see marriage as valuable because of its *symbolic significance* (rather than the add-ons). They're interested in its status *as a tradition* – and this, interestingly, pushes its problematic past to the fore. It's not something that can be ignored.

Think of the symbolism that runs throughout the wedding ceremony. The father-of-the-bride 'gives away' his daughter. But in the normal course of things, we only give away things we own and we don't tend to own people. The officiating priest tells the groom he 'may now kiss the bride'. But the bride's wishes are not considered – she's given no opportunity to decline.

What about the white dress, which is supposed to symbolize the bride's virginity? Women, says the dress, should not have sex before marriage. That seems ill-advised, not to say unfair – especially since the same rule is not applied to men. And think about the traditional exclusion of same-sex couples, which is closely woven into the heterosexist fabric of the wedding rites.

When people marry because they value the tradition, it appears to follow that they value these troubling symbolic associations. This is why philosophers like Clare Chambers and Elizabeth Brake suggest we should reassess our attitude towards marriage. As the title of her essay indicates, Chambers advocates a 'marriage-free state'. By constructing new legal arrangements, we can, she says, get the benefits of the add-ons (parties, taxbreaks, etc) without any of the symbolic violence. Brake's position is slightly different. In her book, *Minimalizing Marriage (2011)*, she encourages us to retain the term 'marriage' but to use it subversively to apply to all legal-bound, caring adult relationships.

Marriage is an old and well-recognized institution. As a tradition, it's popular and pervasive. The questions Chambers and Brake encourage us to ask ourselves are, should it be? And what could we put in its place?

MAKING BABIES

There's no denying it: with their squishy faces and tiny hands, babies can be pretty adorable. Sure, they have downsides – they can't talk, or use toilets and are prone to vomiting – but on the whole, we like them. In fact, a lot of people like them so much, they try and make their own.

It's not hard to see why humans are such big fans of procreation. For one thing, we've been doing it since … well, forever. Since the Year Dot. It can be the product of a famously pleasurable pastime – and it's sort of expected, isn't it? Like dying, creating your own child is seen to be an inevitable part of human life. Find a partner, make a baby. That's just how it goes. Plus they're cute. Did I mention that already?

People love babies – and philosophers, unsurprisingly, love to talk about them.

Take, for instance, the superbly titled B.U.M.P. project (Better Understanding the Metaphysics of Pregnancy) at the University of Southampton. Set up in 2016, Elselijn Kingma's research group looks at the metaphysical puzzles that pregnancy creates. Is a foetus a part of its mother? What about an egg? At what point do these things become distinct entities? At what point does the baby actually come into existence?

There's also the epistemological angle. What puzzles do pregnancy and procreation raise for the production of knowledge? In her fascinating paper 'Mother Knows Best', Fiona Woollard persuasively suggests that women who have experienced pregnancy have a privileged sort of knowledge that others lack. Woollard says that the phenomenology of the event is special. There's no other phenomenon quite like 'the mystery of living with two heartbeats knocking out their rhythms' (as Chitra Ramaswamy puts it in her book *Expecting*, 2016). Pregnancy is a mind-expanding experience.

The epistemology of pregnancy also leads us into the sphere of ethics. A central claim in Woollard's essay is that, by virtue of their unique perspective, mothers have a particular contribution to make to political debates about pregnancy. There's something relevant that these women know, which other people don't, that bears on how abortion is debated. If you don't know what it's like to be pregnant, how can you ask someone to remain pregnant against their will? How can men have informed opinions about such things?

Mothers are giving birth all around us, all the time – around 353,000 every single day – and it's easy, perhaps, to forget how wonderful and fascinating this actually is. You're somewhere, reading this, and POP, there's another baby, and POP there's another one, and POP another – and isn't that incredible? And a little bit overwhelming?

EXISTENCE PROBLEMS

Babies are cute, and pregnancy is obviously philosophically intriguing. But are there any ethical puzzles about the biological creation of an infant? Philosophers Tina Rulli and David Benatar, and Queer theorist Lee Edelman, would answer that there are.

In his book *No Future* (2004), Edelman suggests that the reasons we typically give for procreating usually have little to do with the baby itself. Consider why you might want to create your own child. Well, you may say, babies are adorable. Plus, having a son or daughter can give your life meaning. It changes your perspective on the world. Having a baby is also a profound expression of love for your partner (you love them so much you want your DNA to meld together!) All well and good, but these reasons configure the baby *instrumentally*. That is, this imagined baby is seen as a means to an end – be it the enhancement of your life, or your partner's or of society in general.

When we think about having babies, we can't help but think of them in instrumental terms. Why? *Because they don't exist* (we'll talk more about existence in Chapter 3). Their hopes and desires can't figure in our decision to procreate because nonexistent things don't have hopes and desires. Imagine prospective parents telling you what their future baby will want from life – to be a doctor, say. That would feel odd, because

there's nothing to which the desires can be ascribed! It's not surprising, then, that when it comes to procreation, the focus shifts onto the hopes and desires of existent things (like ourselves).

Tina Rulli, a philosopher at the University of California, encourages us to spend more time thinking about *existing* children. In her article 'The Ethics of Procreation and Adoption' (2016), she points out that there are kids up for adoption or fostering, whose lives would be immeasurably improved by having the stable home you're thinking of providing for your as-yet-nonexistent offspring. There is, she proposes, a relatively uncontroversial moral obligation to look after people who are already suffering rather than to create new people for you to invest these energies in. It's not rocket science: if you've got a sad baby and can help it, why would you focus on creating a completely new baby?

There are obviously more dimensions to this discussion, but the question raised is an important one. Why would you biologically create your own child rather than foster or adopt? Is it because you want a baby that looks like you? Is it because you're naturally inclined to procreate? Are you worried that foster kids are somehow 'damaged'? Do any of these reasons really trump Rulli's moral principle that it's better to care for the living than create a new recipient for your love?

CAN YOU BE
TO DO SOME
THAT IT'S N
POSSIBLE T

EXPECTED
THING
OT
O DO?

EATING MEAT

In the 1970s, the Australian moral philosopher Peter Singer wrote a book called *Animal Liberation: A New Ethics for Our Treatment of Animals* (1975). It quickly became one of the most well-known and influential philosophical texts of the 20th century. One of the reasons for this was an argument Singer includes about hamburgers.

Okay, fine, the argument isn't *just* about hamburgers – it's about a bunch of other tasty foodstuffs too. Chicken nuggets. Roast duck, veal and caviar. Beef, meat loaf and bacon. It's an argument that says we should stop eating them.

Singer takes his philosophical lead from the 18th-century social reformer, Jeremy Bentham – one of the founders of the philosophical movement known as

utilitarianism. The central utilitarian principle, which Singer commends, is that we should do whatever *causes the greatest good* and *minimizes the most suffering*. That's a fairly straightforward rule of thumb, isn't it? Suffering is wrong – and minimizing it seems like a good idea.

Singer's main innovation was to couple this moral principle with a critique of something called 'speciesism' – the prejudice displayed by certain species (mentioning no names, *Homo sapiens*...) against beings of other species. It's not hard to be impressed, like Singer, by the idea prevalent in Algonquin and Iñupiaq culture, that humans are part of a continuum in nature just as much as other animals. There's no *real* reason, says Singer, for us to think of ourselves as having any

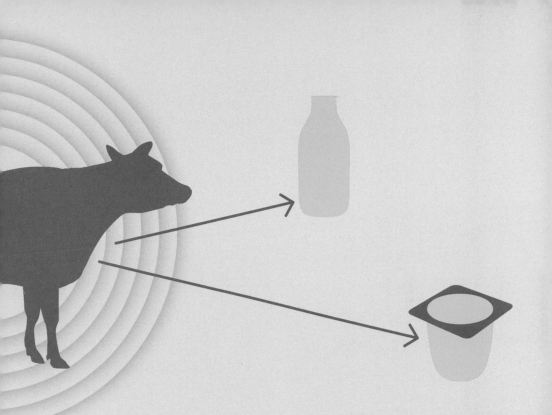

particular privileges because of the species to which we belong. And this applies in the moral sphere as much as any other.

His thought, then, is that nonhuman animals shouldn't be treated like 'wind-up clocks' (despite what the Cartesians say). They feel *pain*, they feel *pleasure*. They can *suffer*. And their capacity for suffering is morally relevant. When we're doing our utilitarian equations, totting up the good and bad, we need to factor in the suffering of cows and sheep and all the other creatures we serve for dinner.

'The question', as Bentham himself put it, 'is not, "Can they reason? Can they talk?" but, "Can they suffer?"' The answer, Singer thinks, is an emphatic *YES*. And it's difficult to disagree. Many of us have seen those gut-churning documentaries about how hamburgers are made. How fish are farmed. The horrible living conditions of battery chickens. The butchering of cattle. Of course, we derive a certain amount of pleasure from eating meat – but it isn't, Singer thinks, nearly enough to weigh the balance in favour of the brutalizing of nonhuman animals.

There are points for and against Singer's position, and as he points out himself, his argument has been considerably less effective than he'd hoped (just look at the continued expansion of the fast-food industry). Still, there remains something profoundly powerful about the ideas fleshed out in *Animal Liberation* – and something disturbing about how easily we exclude beings of other species from our moral calculations.

HOW COME YOU'RE NOT A VEGAN?

One question vegetarians routinely get asked is, *How come you're not a vegan?* – which is, it must be said, a rather irritating thing to ask. Unfortunately, like a lot of irritating things, it's also quite important. The utilitarian principle seen to motivate vegetarianism also goes beyond it.

The dairy industry is – by Singer's reasoning – almost as bad as the meat industry. For instance, cows only produce milk once they've given birth, so they have to have babies once a year to keep lactating. *Once a year!* Can you imagine? Furthermore, all of the male calves are killed and (at best) ground down into mincemeat (and at worst ... well, it's better not to ask). If I want to minimize animal suffering, I have to stop drinking milk and eating cheese and yoghurt as well.

And the problems don't stop there.

Veganism brings its own issues. Vegans need protein – and with cheese and meat off the menu, they'll turn to nuts to get their recommended daily allowance. But the nut industry is susceptible to just as many problems as the meat and milk industries. Take almonds: they require a huge amount of water to grow, and extensive water re-direction can (and does) lead to widespread drought in almond-growing communities. On top of that, not all countries have the climate for nut-growing, so supermarkets have to ship them in – and, guess what? The fumes from boats and planes are contributing to global warming.

When you've got too much on your ethical plate, it's good to remember a lesson learned from Onora O'Neill: *ought implies can.* We want to be good people. We have moral codes and these codes tell us what things we ought to do. But the suggestion that we ought to stop harming animals only makes sense if it's *possible* for us to stop harming animals. We can't be expected to do things that it's not possible for us to do.

Given how most of us live, given the kinds of shop-bought things we wear and eat and use, it's difficult (if not impossible) to be sure whether animal suffering has been a by-product of their manufacture. It would be a full-time job mapping out the causal chain that resulted in the making of this sandwich, or that chocolate bar – it's just not practically possible.

This doesn't, however, mean that we should just give up. The wonderful Ruth Barcan Marcus, in an essay titled 'Moral Dilemmas and Consistency' (1980), describes a 'second order regulative principle'. Roughly speaking, this principle holds that instead of trying, impossibly, to meet all these various moral demands (which will result in moral burn-out, if not outright conflict), we have a responsibility to get ourselves into a position where it's possible to address these concerns. You don't want to be the cause of needless animal suffering, but you only have finite resources to prevent this from happening. You should invest these resources wisely, she says. You should use practical judgement so that your moral practice can become sustainable.

Living a moral life isn't simply a matter of deciding which things you should and shouldn't do. It's a matter of building a lifestyle around these aims. Not all of them will be immediately achievable. You may think it's better to be a vegan than a vegetarian, but it may well take some time researching delicious oat-based milk substitutes before you can finally fulfil this ambition.

SHOPPING

'A commodity appears, at first sight, a very trivial thing, and easily understood. Its analysis shows that it is, in reality, a very queer thing, abounding in metaphysical subtleties and theological niceties.'

That's Marx. Karl, not Groucho. He's talking about iPads and sofas and frisbees and novelty hats and those tiny figurines you get in Kinder Eggs and the Kinder Eggs too. He's talking about *commodities* – those everyday items we put in our houses our cars and our places of work – all commodities.

Marx, the 19th-century Prussian-born philosopher and economist, spent a huge amount of time thinking about these ostensibly ordinary objects. The quote above comes from the first chapter of his magnum opus, *Capital: Critique of Political Economy* (1867), in which he describes the economic models underpinning what he saw as 'capitalist' society. It's a hefty tome, jam-packed with novel thoughts – but for present purposes, we're just going to look at his view of these supposedly 'trivial' things.

A commodity, roughly speaking, is something you can buy, which has been produced by human labour. That's pretty vague, isn't it? It includes cups and saucers, but also computer programs, and more abstract things, like an hour with a management consultant or a package holiday to the Maldives.

Commodities, according to Marx, have two distinct properties. On the one hand, they have 'use value'. The use value of something like a wooden spoon relates to what you can do with it (use it for stirring, say). They also have 'exchange value'. What can you exchange a spoon for? In ye olde days, we might have exchanged a well-carved spoon for a duck or a brace of turnips. Nowadays, we're more likely to exchange it for an hour or two's hard graft in the office through the medium of money. You get paid a certain amount for your labour and you use the money you earn to buy a beautiful spoon.

For Marx, the focus in a capitalist economy is very much on the latter of these two values. Capitalists aren't especially interested in what the object is or how it can be used, but in what you can exchange it for and whether or not it will make a profit. The market is geared to that end, the production of profit rather than the production of useful items ... which is probably why there's so much stuff around the place.

Marx says that, at first blush, commodities seem 'trivial' and 'easily understood'. Take this book, for example: you've seen others like it, and irrespective of the content, it probably doesn't — as an object — hold any special fascination for you. You certainly don't consider it an odd thing. The same goes for tables and chairs, and so on and so forth. We think of commodities as humdrum, everyday items.

Yet Marx goes on to say these things abound in 'metaphysical subtleties and theological niceties'. They're a lot more mysterious than they first appear. This is a thought that he aims to capture with his notion of 'commodity fetishism'.

We typically associate the word 'fetish' with sexual practices, but in Marx's work the concept of 'fetishism' is one that comes out of ethnographic and anthropological discourse; it refers to the way in which certain objects — like totems or charms — are seen to possess supernatural powers. But what possible powers do commodities have? What strange magic is possessed by our possessions?

Tree

BEHIND THE CURTAIN

Lke all good magical items, commodities *appear out of nowhere*. Most of the time, we see them on the shelves, as though they've just popped into existence. Sure, we're aware people stock the shops, but our thoughts rarely go beyond that. In the normal run of things, we have absolutely no contact with a commodity's *producers*. We don't see them and we certainly don't exchange things with them directly. Long gone are the good old days of turnips and wooden spoons. Indeed, a lot of the time, each commodity (your digital watch, say) is produced by a huge number of people, and these producers themselves rarely see, let alone speak to each other either.

Think of all the various materials that have gone into making this book. The paper, for one thing. The bleach that's turned the paper white, the glue that's glued the spine. The ink, the plastic, or the laminate that gives it a glossy shine. All of these have different origins and yet we engage with the book as a *single, unified object*. In actual fact, it's designed to look like that. The manufacturers have taken incredible care to erase the signs of its production.

We don't think of books as being produced by people. As you're reading this, you're unlikely to be thinking of the hours I've spent sitting at my desk typing out these words, or about how much I'm getting paid. It's unlikely you've thought at all about the working conditions of the designers, the editors, the printers and publishers. Or the foresters who grow the trees that make the paper, or the chemists who've made the pigment to make the ink. These aspects of the book are well and truly hidden – and that's the magic of commodities. We don't see them as the products of human labour. We don't think about the people who made them or about how these people are treated.

At the end of the day, 'commodity fetishism' is not a particularly impressive type of magic. It's like David Copperfield; the producers haven't *actually* disappeared – it's a trick of the light. The often exploitative social relations are still there. In Marx's book *Capital* (1867), he was trying to pull back the curtain to show how we're being duped. The next time you go out to buy something, try and think about its use value, its exchange value and the producers that made it happen.

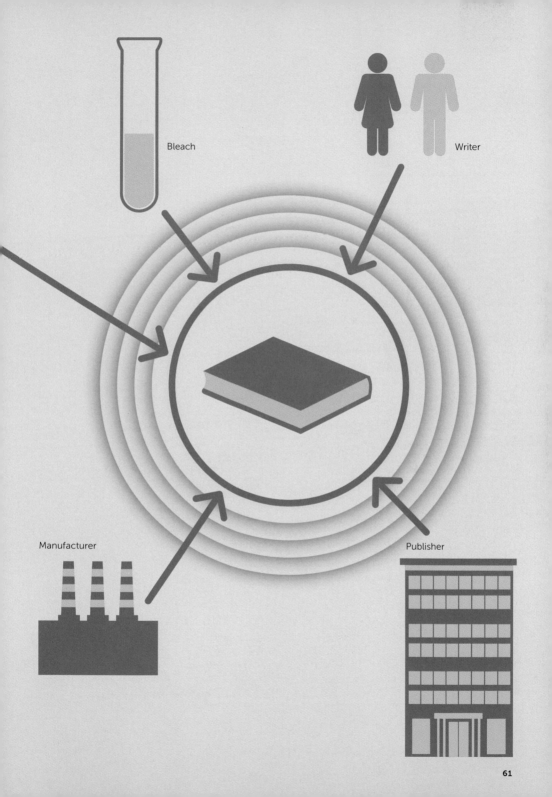

Bleach

Writer

Manufacturer

Publisher

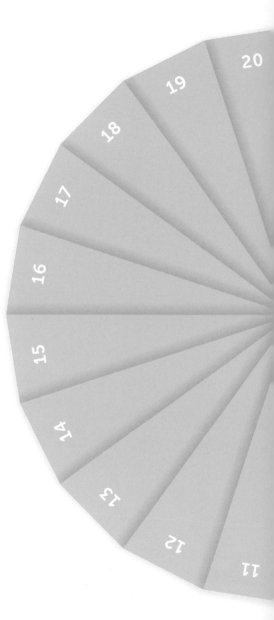

**BUILD +
BECOME**

TOOLKIT

05

The institution of marriage has a disturbing
history. If we celebrate it as a tradition then
it's hard not to celebrate its troubling past.
Thinking point Are there any traditions that
don't have a troubling past?

06

Having children is a wonderful, mind-
expanding experience, but there might be
a moral imperative to look after *existing
children* rather than create *new ones*.
Thinking point Does this mean humans
should stop having babies?

01
02
03
04
05
06
07
08
09
10

07

Animal suffering motivates us to change what we eat. To avoid becoming overwhelmed by ethical demands, we need to recognize our limited personal resources and deploy them sensibly.

Thinking point Can there ever be good reasons to stop yourself caring about injustice?

08

By fixating on the commodity rather than on the means by which it is produced, we tend to forget that many of our everyday purchases are the result of exploitative labour.

Thinking point What do you need to do in order to buy better?

FURTHER LEARNING

READ

We Are What We Eat
Cathryn Bailey, *Hypatia* (2007)

If You're an Egalitarian How Come You're So Rich?
G.A. Cohen (Harvard University Press, 1996)

Exploitation
Nancy Holmstrom, *Canadian Journal of Philosophy* (1977)

WATCH

The Spectre of Marxism
Academic and broadcaster Stuart Hall explores Karl Marx and the history of Marxism in this in-depth BBC documentary from 1983.

Carnage
A fascinating (and often hilarious) fusion of fact and fiction, this docudrama directed by Simon Amstell discusses the impact of meat-eating in the 21st (and 22nd) centuries.

LISTEN

'The Morality of Parental Rights',
The Moral Maze
BBC Radio 4 debate presented by Michael Buerk with Ed Condon, Raanan Gillon, Carol Iddon and Dominic Wilkinson. *The Moral Maze* is one of the BBC's political debate programmes that often features interesting contributions from philosophers.

VISIT

Phil.Cologne
In 2017, over 12,000 people attended the fifth Phil.Cologne festival in Cologne, which speaks to the growing popularity of philosophical discussion in Germany. The organizers do a good job of getting a range of philosophical opinions.

Festival of Questions
Part of the famous Melbourne Festival, the Festival of Questions gathers together politicians, philosophers and comedians to discuss (sometimes provocatively) important issues facing 21st-century Australians.

SELF-HELP

LESSONS

09 STAYING ALIVE
We're all going to die! But what does this mean in
metaphysical terms?

10 THE REAL ME
Who are you *really*? More to the point, *what* are you?
A single, discrete, unified self ... or something less tangible?

11 DEALING WITH DEATH
Can reason actually help us overcome the deaths of our
loved ones? And, more importantly, *should* it?

12 DEATH AND TAXES
What are liberal selves? And why don't they like paying taxes?

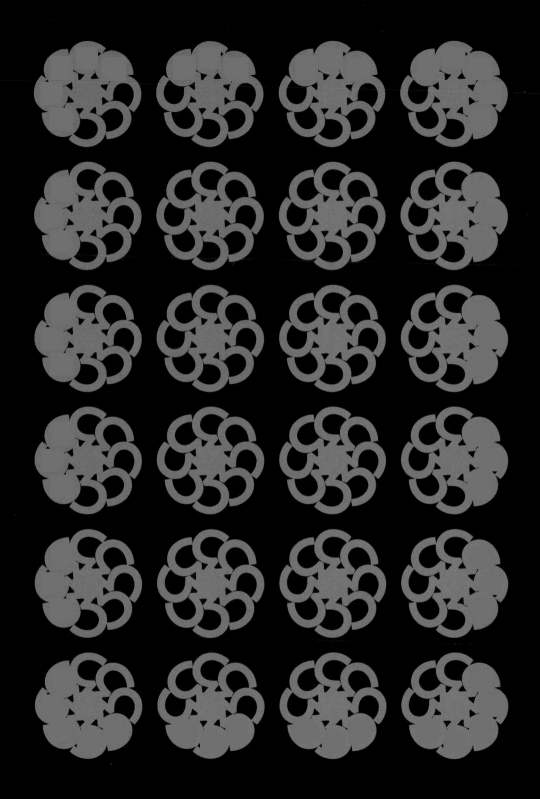

> 'We form ourselves within the vocabularies that we did not choose, and sometimes we have to reject those vocabularies, or actively develop new ones.'
> *Judith Butler*

Who on earth do you think you are? More to the point, what on earth do you think you are? In this chapter, we'll look at the kinds of beings we consider ourselves to be. Are we *animals? Persons?* What about *selves?* We'll also look at some of the issues confronting these kinds of beings (death's a big one!) and examine how we can respond to them.

More often than not, if you hear an anglophone philosopher talking about selves and persons, they're referring to the 'personal identity' debate. This is a strand of thought originating in the 17th century with the philosopher and physician John Locke. Locke wanted to know what it took for beings like himself and his fellows at the Royal Society to survive through space and time. That's the focus of Lesson 9, 'Staying Alive'.

However, as we'll see in the lessons that follow, Locke's position is only one of many. We'll look at Buddhist views of the self (and lack thereof) and Confucian accounts of how to build yourself a true self. We'll begin to break down the idea of a 'natural' you, with instinctive wants and desires. In Lesson 11, we'll also look at how the Epicureans and the Stoics thought we could deal with death of the self – all the while wondering what, exactly, dying actually is. In the final lesson, 'Death and Taxes', we'll see how the idea of a discrete, unified choosing being – a self – plays out in the politics of 'liberalism'.

Warning! If you're prone to bouts of existential angst, or fear of the oceanic feeling, this chapter might not be for you. Side-effects of the following arguments include: dizzy spells, ontological puzzlement, and occasional loss of selfhood.

STAYING ALIVE

There's no easy way to break this to you, but ... well ... you're going to die. Heck, all of us are. But what does it actually mean to say that we're 'going to die'? Does it mean 'going out of existence'? It's a strange thought and will benefit from philosophical extrapolation.

Fortunately, in his *Essay Concerning Human Understanding* (1689), the British philosopher John Locke sets out to examine exactly this. In Book II, Chapter 27, he lays out what he thinks our 'persistence conditions' are – the criteria that must be met for us to continue to exist.

Now, it's easy to outline specific conditions for our survival. We mustn't get squashed by falling pianos, for example. We must avoid drinking deadly poison. We must prevent ourselves from having our heads chopped off. Locke, however, doesn't want a list of the multifarious ways in which we can perish. That would be boring and grisly (and infinite). Rather, he wants to know what the general conditions for survival are. What is it that poisoning, decapitation and being squashed by a piano (etc) have in common?

In order to answer this question, he says, we need to look at the sorts of things that we are (which is why he's sometimes, imaginatively, called a 'sortalist'). Of course, he recognizes we can be all sorts of things – nurses, tailors, soldiers, students and so on – but since we can clearly survive a change in career, we should, he says, fix on the sorts of things that you and I are *fundamentally*.

Maybe, at the end of a day, you're a human – a particular kind of animal, the species *Homo sapiens*. And maybe your survival is a matter of the persistence of this human animal. Or maybe you're an immortal soul? Perhaps you persist so long as this specific immaterial soul persists?

Ultimately, Locke claims that we are fundamentally persons. A person is a 'thinking intelligent being that has reason and reflection, and can consider itself as itself, the same thinking thing in different times and places...' It's a self-conscious, rational, thinking entity that continues through time and space. We might also call it 'a consciousness'.

There are even weirder sci-fi stories out there, about people's personalities being downloaded onto computers and zapped into outer space, but the general intuition that seems to support the Lockean picture is that you survive as long as your particular consciousness survives. 'Continued consciousness' is our number-one persistence condition.

Moreover, Locke helpfully tells us how we can check for continued consciousness: he says we should look to an individual's *memories*. If there's someone who has your memories and remembers doing all the things you've done from a first-person perspective, that's pretty good evidence to show that someone is you.

This, then, is the Lockean account of personal identity. Your survival is not a matter of some human animal persisting (or some immaterial soul wafting along), but of a single thinking person continuing through space and time, as evidenced by continued experiential memory.

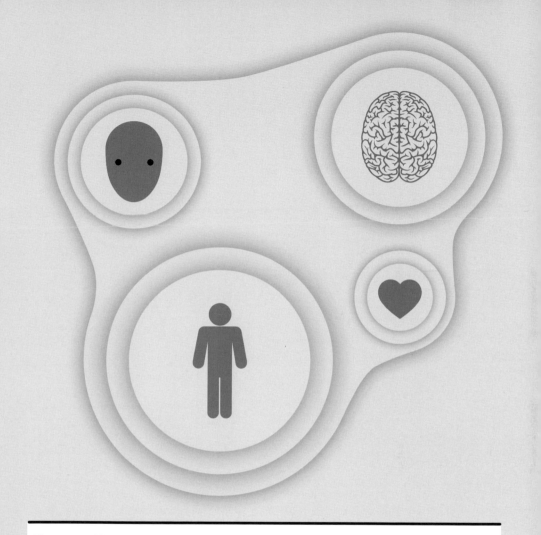

To support his view, Locke and his followers tell stories where beings like you and me seem to survive changes of body or soul specifically because of continued consciousness. The canonical neo-Lockean story is the 'brain transplantation' narrative, told to us by philosopher Sydney Shoemaker in his book *Self-Knowledge and Self-Identity* (1963). Imagine I take out your brain and put it into another prepared head; the patient who wakes may look nothing like you – it's not the same human animal – but it has all of your memories and all of your character traits. So it's the same person. Do you think you'd survive the operation? If you do, Shoemaker says, it's because you identify yourself as a particular consciousness, a particular thinking thing. The human animal that sits where you are currently standing is little more than a vessel for the person you fundamentally are.

DON'T FORGET THE MEMORIES

Most of the time, when it comes to people going out of existence, we don't really need philosophy to tell us what's going on. If you get squashed by a piano, people aren't going to call for a metaphysician – they're going to call for an undertaker. This is because we think, on the whole, that the death of the human animal coincides with the death of the person; when the heart stops beating and 'brain death' occurs, a particular consciousness (sadly) stops as well.

But there are problem cases too. Ignoring the peculiar philosophical fantasies (brain transplantations, character downloads, tele-transportations and so on), we can tell more mundane and more troublesome stories that cause us to question what we think we are and what it takes for us to survive.

Think about a human life. The life of Hamid. Hamid starts off as a foetus, before being born as a cute baby. He grows into a troublesome toddler, then becomes a thoughtful teenager and an intelligent young man. He grows older and then, sadly, in his late seventies he begins to suffer from dementia. On his eightieth birthday, Hamid contracts pneumonia and is placed in a medically induced coma. Shortly afterwards his vital functions stop and he dies. This, we think, is a complete life.

On the Lockean account, however, Hamid exists for only a part of it. Remember, Locke thinks that we are, fundamentally, *thinking things*. But is the foetus that Hamid once was *self-conscious*? Does Hamid have memories of his mother's womb? And what about dementia? He forgets who he is and who his family members are. His character changes dramatically. Is he the same person he was as a teenager? The Lockean might have cause for doubt – and that seems a strangely hard-line response to a subtle, disturbing and commonplace situation. And if the person can survive dementia, can it survive the coma as well, from which Hamid never wakes?

There are lots of cases – from amnesia to vegetative-state patients – that put pressure on the Lockean account of personal identity. We think, of course, that consciousness is an important part of one's being, but is it the *most fundamental* part? Your views on this can have far-reaching consequences. In the debate on abortion, for instance, you might think it relevant whether or not we're fundamentally *human animals* (who come in existence at conception) or *persons* (who come into existence much later). When you're writing your will, you might want to specify how you'd like to be treated if you end up in an irreversible coma; if you think you're a person, then you may not identify with the vegetative patient on the life-support machine.

Most of the time, we don't need philosophy to tell us what's going on – but sometimes a philosophical analysis helps us understand what we want to do, how we want to be treated and why.

THE REAL ME

Self-help. It's a term you see around a lot these days. The industry is thriving. All across the media spectrum, we're encouraged to help our inner selves by shopping and weight loss and smiling and enemas and goodness knows what else. And of course, all these books and television programmes and apps can be helpful. But what exactly are they helping? Is it your *self*? Some clear determinate *you*, replete with hopes, dreams and desires?

In the previous lesson, 'Staying Alive', we looked at the person – the me, the I, the thing you think of as <insert your name here>. We played with the idea that there is some thing that you think you are fundamentally. A 'true self', a being that is conscious of 'itself', that thinks, wills, makes decisions, has wants and needs, and so on. It's an idea with considerable pedigree. It appeals to us. It makes sense.

But what if it's all hokum? What if there is no real, substantial self or person who directs your actions and generates your desires? What if, when you look deep inside, you find ... nothing? Nada? Zip?

This idea, that there isn't really a real me, isn't a particularly new one. Some of the most sophisticated discussions of 'egolessness' emerge out of the Buddhist tradition, which dates from the 4th century BC. According to the Buddhist monk Nyanatiloka Mahathera:

'The Buddha teaches that what we call ego, self, soul, personality, etc, are merely conventional terms not referring to any real independent entity. And he teaches that there is only to be found this psychophysical process of existence changing from moment to moment ... This doctrine of egolessness of existence forms the essence of the Buddha's doctrine of emancipation. Thus with this doctrine of egolessness, or *annatta*, stands or falls the entire Buddhist structure.'

Nor is the critique of the apparently 'natural' ego restricted to the Buddhist tradition. Sociologists and philosophers from Marcel Mauss to N. Katherine Hayles have shown how the emphasis on a sovereign self is socioculturally located. Our fascination with the 'self' is a product of a particular type of society. In more precise terms, the political scientist C.B. Macpherson suggests that the idea of an autonomous self achieves the prominence it does because of its position in political liberalism (which we'll look at in Lesson 12).

Have a think. Turn inwards. See if you can see yourself. What are the things that make you, *you*? Is there really a coherent entity there? Or is it just a stream of thoughts, bundled up together like a big ball of lint? This sentence floats by ... and the next moment, what's that? A memory of a romantic dalliance. A daydream. The smell of roast potatoes. Look deeper. Are your hopes and dreams anything more than fleeting thoughts? Where did they come from, why do you have them? Did you choose to have the hopes you have?

Are you dizzy yet?

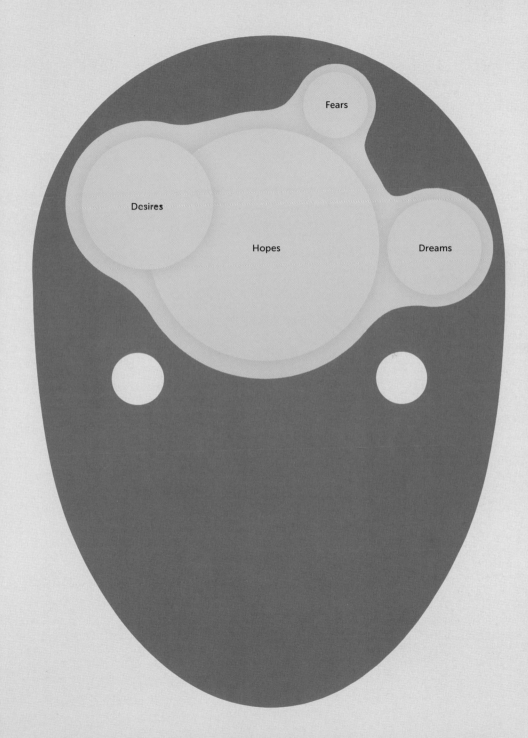

BUILD YOURSELF A SELF

It appears we should be slightly more circumspect when it comes to our *selves*. The idea of a fully formed inner being is, perhaps, somewhat shady. Maybe what you think of as *your true self* is in fact nothing more than a bundle of learned behaviours, chemically induced emotions and stimulus-response reactions. There are experiences that go on in this blob of flesh – cold, heat, pain, pleasure, etc – but they're not had by any coherent entity. We interact with things and react, but our reactions are no more meaningful or self-directed than those of a daffodil leaning towards the sun.

If you're worried by these thoughts, you may find some solace in the teachings of the Chinese philosopher Confucius. At roughly the same time that the Buddha was spreading his teachings in northern India, and Socrates was causing trouble in Greece, the politician-cum-editor-cum-polymath Confucius was tackling the problem of egolessness in the the ancient Lu state of China. Fortunately for us, his work is currently enjoying something of a renaissance in the West, thanks to excellent research by Michael Puett and Christine Gross-Loh.

According to Confucius we are, ultimately, just messy bundles of emotions. There's no guiding 'self' that commands your life. So far, so familiar. But in the *Analects*, Confucius also appears to suggest that we have the potential to *build* ourselves a self.

How? Well, the first step is to challenge learned behaviours. Most of our lives are taken up with standard stimulus-response reactions. Think, for example, of the last time someone asked how you were feeling

– chances are you said 'Fine', right? How often do you make small talk about the weather? What other habits do you have? When was the last time there was *genuine engagement*? Confucius calls us to question these behaviours through enacting *rituals.* As Gross-Loh and Puett put it in *The Path* (2016):

'Rituals – in the Confucian sense – are transformative because they allow us to become a different person for a moment. They create a short-lived alternate reality that returns us to our regular life slightly altered. For a brief moment, we are living in an "as-if" world.'

Rather than reinforcing restrictive habits, rituals allow us to break out of certain structures through a form of *role-playing.*

Take, for instance, ritual fasting, which is common to many religions. There are various reasons for this sort of asceticism, but whether for Yom Kippur, Lent or Ramadan, deprivation of this sort puts you in the position of someone less fortunate than yourself. It's an 'as-if' scenario. You're behaving as if you don't have enough food to eat. Munching through three meals a day is something you likely do without thinking. The ritual of fasting challenges the conventions of breakfast, lunch and dinner, and encourages you to think more about this learned behaviour. By engaging in this ritual, you're jolted out of autopilot. You're encouraged to pay attention, to engage genuinely. You actively make decisions. You stop being a daffodil. And in doing so, according to Confucius, you start to build a self.

DID YOU CH
TO HAVE TH
YOU HAVE?

DOSE
E HOPES

DEALING WITH DEATH

Are you afraid of death? Don't worry, most of us are. Irrespective of your views about human persistence, it's hard not to worry about popping your clogs, or kicking the bucket, or whatever your preferred euphemism is. The worry seems especially keen for folk who don't believe in an afterlife.

For Plato, philosophy is a practice that helps people prepare for death. It's an intellectual tradition that allows you to come to terms with your impending demise. And the Athenian philosopher Epicurus, who lived a century or so after Plato, is well known for trying to follow up on this premise. When faced with the all-consuming fear of mortality, his advice was to chill the heck out – and think rationally. The argument paraphrased below appears in a letter he wrote to his buddy Menoeceus.

Consider the following premise: *Death is annihilation*. When something dies, it's annihilated. That is, it *goes out of existence*. We're left with nothing (or, in the Latin, *nihil*). Living beings, like you and me, have not been annihilated – otherwise we wouldn't be alive (obviously). So it seems fair to say that death (which is annihilation) does not affect the living. Death, therefore, can't be *bad* for the living, since the living don't experience it.

And – get this – death isn't bad for dead people either! Because for something to be bad for someone, that person has to, at the very least, *exist*. The dead (as we've seen) do not exist. They've been annihilated. So according to Epicurus, death is neither bad for the living nor the dead. Take that, death!

A century or so after Epicurus, the Roman poet Lucretius came along and offered a supplement to this line of reasoning, called the 'symmetry argument'. In *De Rerum Natura*, Lucretius pointed out that the type of nonexistence that results from death appears to be suspiciously similar in character to the type of nonexistence associated with birth. He points out that since we spend little to no time worrying about the pre-birth, it makes no sense to worry about the 'after-life':

'Look back now and consider how the bygone ages of eternity that elapsed before our birth were nothing to us. Here, then, is a mirror in which nature shows us the time to come after our death. Do you see anything fearful in it? Do you perceive anything grim? Does it not appear more peaceful than the deepest sleep?'

According to these ancient philosophers, it's completely illogical to be scared of death. So why does it still unsettle us?

Birth

Existence

Death

DEAD LETTERS

'When she died I no longer wished to live, neither could I find any comfort from the dull dictates of Philosophy, which was then as a dead Letter.'

These are the words of the 18th-century philosopher Jenny Harry, talking about the death of her sister. The point she's making is an important one. Even if the arguments we find in Epicurus and Lucretius help us confront our own deaths, they do little to comfort us when it comes to the death of a loved one. The symmetry argument might be fine and dandy, persuasive even in the abstract, but it offers small consolation to bereaved family members. In these contexts, philosophy is little more than a 'dead Letter'. It's useless.

Indeed, there's something almost disturbing about the idea of using a philosophical thesis to counter such harrowing experiences. The grief we feel when a parent or sibling dies is utterly appropriate. It's bizarre to think we should try and reason it away – and it's hubristic for philosophers to suggest that they can. Death of a loved one can't be squared away like an equation. It's not a puzzle to be solved.

Jenny Harry writes that the most philosophy could do 'was to sink the mind into a state of apathy'. She appears to be referring to the ancient idea of *apatheia*, advocated by the Greek Stoics.

Stoicism is a form of Hellenistic philosophy, presently making something of a return to the philosophical scene (with an international 'Stoic week' and even a convention called 'Stoicon'). *Apatheia*, or apathy, is one of its central philosophical principles: the idea is that you should cultivate *indifference* in order to protect yourself from unpleasant emotions that disturb tranquillity.

Jenny Harry, perhaps understandably, wasn't much impressed by this tactic. Nor is Richard Sorabji who, in his book *Emotion and Peace of Mind* (2000), criticizes Stoicism on precisely these grounds. The Stoic, he says, believes that we should nurture indifference because, in the grand scheme of things, nothing is really good or evil, just preferable from a particular standpoint.

'[But] it is better to treat the welfare of our loved ones as something very much more than rightly preferred, even though the Stoics are right that this means incurring the risk of loss and desolation...'

It may be that apathy protects us from desolation, but the cost, as Sorabji points out, is high. Harry is searching for something to comfort her – to help her see the point in living – but the best she can find in philosophy is apathy. Apathy guards us from painful emotions, but it also walls us off from joy and solace. Harry eventually finds comfort in Christianity, and in the belief in an afterlife rather than 'the folly of metaphysical reasoning'. Not everyone will want to take this course, but Harry succeeds in drawing important attention to the limited application of philosophy's often arid rationality.

DEATH AND TAXES

Nothing in life is certain except for death and taxes – so said the American politician and philosopher Benjamin Franklin. And of the two, people sometimes add, death is preferable.

Property tax, consumption tax, inheritance tax; we're taxed on food, on houses, on clothes, on holidays, even on *death* itself. We're taxed in pretty much every area of our lives – often large amounts of money – so it's not surprising when folk are less than thrilled about submitting tax returns. We spend our time scrimping and saving, and it grates just a little (or more than a little) when the taxman takes a cut. Taxation is a financial restriction on our personal endeavours, we say, on our lives. It's just one of the many areas in which the state intervenes in our private affairs. And sometimes, maybe more than sometimes, it goes *too far.*

If you think taxation is *over the top*, that the government interferes *too much*, then you might be what political philosophers call a 'political liberal'.

The word 'liberal' has different meanings. It can mean 'open-minded'. 'Anita's very liberal when it comes to parenting' – that suggests Anita is non-traditional with respect to parenting. 'Liberal' also means 'generous', as in, 'apply BBQ sauce liberally'. If you say you're a *political liberal*, however, that means you identify with a particular political tradition, one that came to global prominence during and after the American and French Revolutions in the 18th century.

In his illuminating essay, 'Liberalism, Individuality, and Identity' (2001), Kwame Anthony Appiah draws out some of the philosophical ideas that informed this tradition. Grounded in the work of John Locke (from Lesson 9), *liberalism* (sometimes *libertarianism*) is characterized by a focus on personal *liberty* and *equality*.

The liberal says that every person should be free – at *liberty* – to do what they want, so long as this doesn't impact negatively on another person's liberty. If you want to eat donuts for breakfast, go for it! If you want to steal from your neighbour … *don't go for it.*

Liberalism also configures every person as *equal* to every other. Equal with respect to what, exactly? With respect to *respect*. As possessors of human dignity, each of us is entitled to the same shares of respect. 'We all come into and go out of the world in much the same way,' says Appiah; we're all equally dignified, so none of us should be accorded more respect than any other.

If you're a political liberal, then, you're probably going to want to live in a *republic* rather than a *monarchy* (because kings and queens consider themselves better than everyone else). You're also going to want *minimal state intervention*. You won't want your personal life to be subject to governmental interference. Sure, you'll let it manage regulatory bodies – like the police – to stop people stealing from each other (and that might require minimal taxation). But other than that, you should be allowed to go about your business in the way you see fit. The state shouldn't tax you to fund nonessential projects. It's not up to them where to invest your hard-earned cash. So says the liberal.

So which do *you* prefer? Death or taxes? Your money or your life?

EXAMINE YOURSELF LIBERALLY

'If there were a word for the consensus within which electoral politics is debated in the industrialized world today, it may as well be liberalism'.

Perhaps Appiah's claim explains our universal grouchiness about paying taxes – yet even the political liberal thinks taxation is necessary for regulatory purposes (to fund the police and judiciary, and so forth).

On reflection, we might think the state should tax us for other services as well. Take national health care. It's a good idea – even though it falls outside the ambit of what the liberal state should do. The same is true of state welfare, which protects members of society who can't protect themselves. The political liberal, however, doesn't think this should be the state's job. If a person wants to give money, privately, to charity, they can, but it should be *their* individual choice.

In 'Liberalism, Individuality, and Identity', Appiah puts pressure on what some might see to be this self-serving side of liberalism. And his objections emerge out of a metaphysical and political discussion.

Remember John Locke? In Lesson 9 we saw how fascinated he was by the concept of a *person*. In his *Essay Concerning Human Understanding*, he construed a person as a single, discrete entity, with its own distinctive desires. There's no blurriness between persons, said Locke; you're you, I'm me, and never the twain shall meet (metaphysically speaking).

Appiah – like some of the other philosophers in this chapter – is wary of this Lockean picture. Drawing on the work of Michel Foucault and Charles Taylor, he suggests that every person, every self, is created 'dialogically': through *dialogue* with others – friends and family, and broader society. The self, says Appiah, is 'not some authentic inner essence independent of the human world into which we have grown – but rather the product of our interaction from our earliest years with others'.

Think about your personal ambitions. Where did they come from? Did you think them up by yourself? Or were they conceived in conversation with parents, teachers and friends? With books, with films, with music? With other members of society? The Lockean idea of a discrete person, with a complete set of vacuum-packed desires, lies at the heart of political liberalism. But it's metaphysically confused. Your identity, your selfhood, is inextricably connected with those of your fellow humans. So, Appiah says, the liberal thought that the self should be prioritized over sociability is poorly conceived.

This may not make paying your taxes any more palatable ... but it might, at least, make it more metaphysically coherent.

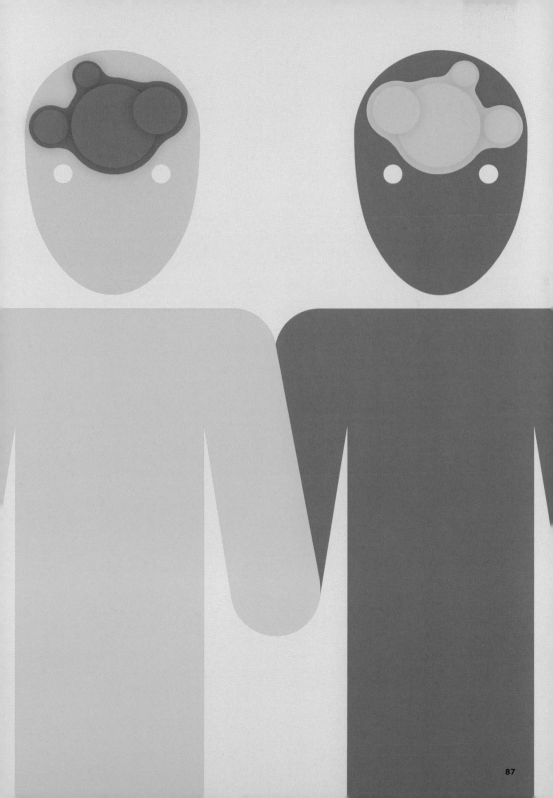

BUILD +
BECOME

TOOLKIT

09

Neo-Lockeans claim that we're persons, or
consciousnesses. 'Animalists' say that we are,
more fundamentally, human animals.
Thinking point Is there something wrong
with being fundamentally two different things
at the same time?

10

Buddhist philosophy encourages us to
question the idea of a natural self. Confucius
suggests that we can build our selves up by
practising rituals.
Thinking point Is it possible to formulate the
claim that you don't have a self?

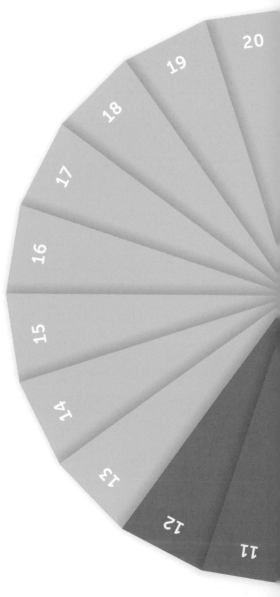

01
02
03
04
05
06
07
08
09
10

11

Epicurus says that if you're dead, you can't experience suffering, so you shouldn't be afraid of death. This attempt to rationalize our emotions is unsatisfying.
Thinking point Is death scarier for atheists or for people who believe in Hell?

12

Political liberalism prizes individual liberty and equality.
Thinking point Are there ever cases when someone's rights to certain freedoms (like freedom of speech) conflict with the aims of an egalitarian society?

FURTHER LEARNING

READ

'Feminism in Philosophy of Mind: the Question of Personal Identity'
Susan James, in *The Cambridge Companion to Feminism in Philosophy* (Cambridge University Press, 2000)

'Mistresses of Their Own Destiny: Group Rights, Gender, and Realistic Rights of Exit'
Susan Okin, *Ethics* (2002)

The Therapy of Desire
Martha Nussbaum (Princeton University Press, 1994)

LISTEN

'Like a Rolling Stone: Stoic Ethics' (Episode 63), History of Philosophy Without Any Gaps
Another wonderful online resource for learning about the history of philosophy, presented by Peter Adamson. Engaging and accessible – definitely worth a listen.

WATCH

Born in Flames
This movie, directed by Lizzie Borden, has to be seen to be believed – an amazing sci-fi docudrama that examines identity politics and liberalism with humour and insight.

Unknown White Male
Documentary filmmaker Rupert Murray focuses on the life of his friend, Doug Bruce, who suffers from severe amnesia – with contributions from the philosopher Mary Warnock.

8-bit Philosophy, Wisecrack
Tune in on YouTube to see philosophy explained through classic retro video games.

VISIT

Stoicon
Stoics from around the world meet at this annual international event to discuss how the tenets of Stoic philosophy can be applied to everyday life.
www.modernstoicism.com/stoicon-stoicism-conference/

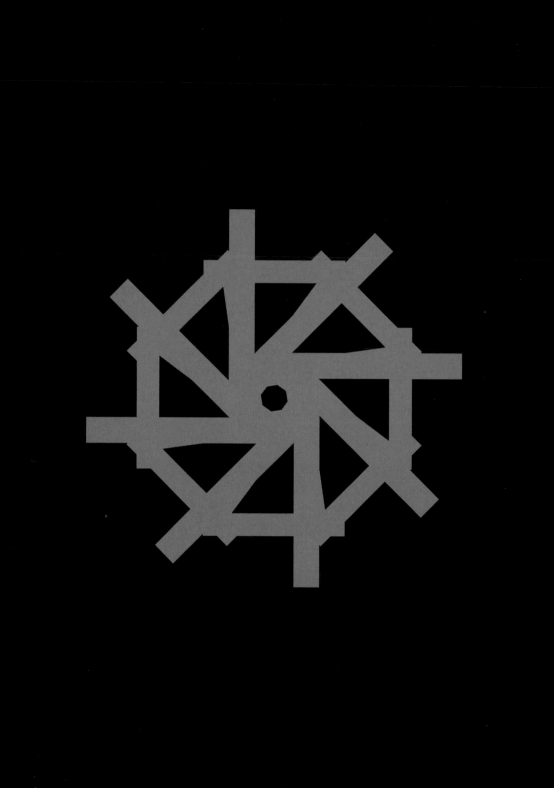

SOCIETY

LESSONS

13 GROUP MENTALITY
We often group people according to biological sex or race
– but how real are these apparently 'natural' categories?

14 CLUB RULES
There are unspoken, invisible rules that structure society.
Some of us see them, some don't. Do you?

15 MAKING AMENDS
We tend to think that we're only responsible for crimes we
commit ourselves. But what about the ones we benefit from?

16 MORAL RUBBISH
Can you effectively respond to a climate-change sceptic
without invoking science? Short answer: yes.

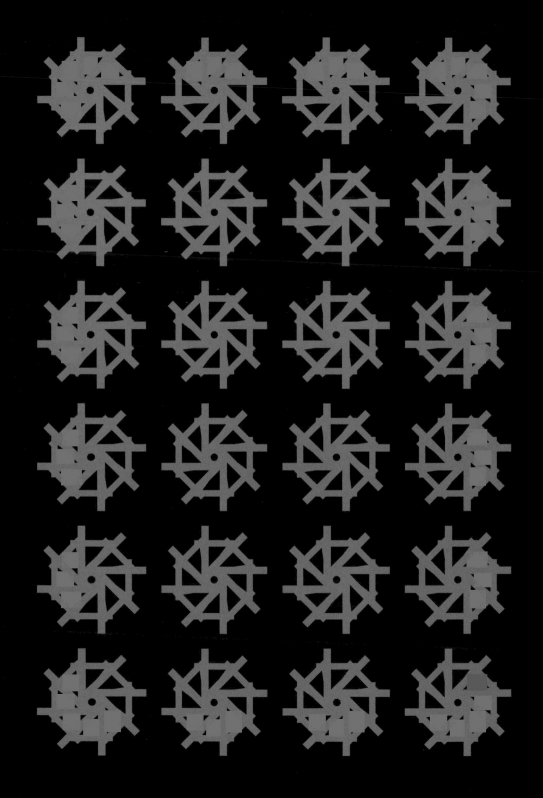

'The success of a society is to be evaluated primarily by the freedoms that members of that society enjoy.'
Amartya Sen

Humans are social beings. We live with other humans – in the same house, on the same street, in the same village, town or city. Our lives are deeply interconnected. We form lasting relationships and rely on each other for food, shelter and help with the plumbing. We live in a society and it is this peculiar entity – the 'society' – that is the subject of the present chapter.

Minimally, a society is a group of people. More often than not, this group is made up of other groups. A lot of societies are composed of numerous smaller communities divided along, for example, religious or geographical lines. The focus of Lesson 13, 'Group Mentality', is on our ways of drawing group boundaries. Are some groups more 'natural' than others? Are nationalities legitimate groups? Does it make sense to split people up according to biological sex or race?

Much of the time, we don't really examine why we arrange people in certain ways. It seems inevitable ... until we bring philosophy to bear. Philosophers try to examine the hidden reasons behind these groupings. In 'Club Rules', we'll look at the invisible laws that organize society – the background ideas, or 'ideologies', that shape the way we live.

We'll also look at how we function as *members* of societies. You might think you're only responsible for the actions you consciously take yourself. But can we take responsibility *as a group*? In 'Making Amends', we'll look at reasons for thinking we might. Lastly, in Lesson 16, we'll examine how our group actions, as a global society, are endangering the planet – and why it's better to bet on climate change rather than to assume it isn't happening.

As ever, the hope isn't to solve these problems. We want to ask questions about the questions they raise – and the chapter will finish with a few further puzzles raised by the puzzles within it.

GROUP MENTALITY

Remember at school how everyone used to separate into *cliques*? The cool kids, the nerdy kids, the sporty kids? Back then, the boundaries seemed irrevocably fixed, and woe betide anyone who tried to cross them. Growing older, the groups became less clear. You could be a nerd about sport. It could be cool to be nerdy. The cliques formed at school began to look arbitrary.

Still, even in adult life, we like to group people. By nationality, for example. Nationality seems a more substantial basis than 'nerd'. Membership of a nation has *legal foundation*. Membership of the nation of nerds does not. There are other groupings that appear sturdier still. We separate *men* and *women*. We also split people into different *races*. Many social groupings can *appear* to be a straightforward reflection of biological fact. People say, and have said for a long time, that there are clear biological differences between men and women, and

between people of different races. The groupings are *natural*. So race and biological sex are – at least the thought goes – what philosophers call, 'natural kinds'.

To categorize entities into 'natural kinds', is – according to Plato – to 'cut nature at the joints'. In his famous (and grisly) 'butcher' analogy, there are real seams in the world – and one of the tasks of the Natural Philosopher is to find them and carve things out accordingly. This was also an ambition of Immanuel Kant (who we met in Lesson 2) in his 1775 treatise, *On the Different Races of Man*. This unwholesome text is an attempt to classify humans into 'biological' kinds and to order these 'races' into what he saw to be a natural 'hierarchy' – with white people at the top.

As you can see, it's depressingly easy for racial classification – a distinction between supposed racial groups – to blur into racism – a *hierarchy* of racial groups.

Many have criticized Kant for promoting a racial hierarchy – and rightly so – but a growing number of philosophers also criticize him for claiming that races are 'natural kinds' at all. Here we can dip our toes into an ever-expanding pool known as 'philosophy of biology', a central question of which is: *Are these kinds actually natural?* The answer, with respect to both biological sex and biological race, is: not really. We'll focus on race (though for more on sex, see the work of the wonderful Judith Jack Halberstam).

Richard Lewontin is a philosopher of biology who challenges the concept of race on scientific grounds. It's true, he says, that your standard racial markers have a genetic basis – but only minimally true, insofar as skin and hair colour are the result of a specific genetic structure. It's also true that *nobody has ever found a race-distinguishing gene*, such that 100% of one race has it, and none of the others do. Analysis also shows that

genetic variation *within* so-called racial groups is much greater than variation *across* so-called racial groups. Sure, there are *some* genetic similarities (for example sickle-cell anaemia is more prevalent in Mediterranean groups than in the population of Finland), but these are the exceptions rather than the rule.

Then there's the conceptual problem for biologists who want to talk about race. In order to find out which genetic factors link members of a race, you have to first pick out the race. But how do we pick out the race *before* we know who its members are? As Naomi Zack puts it in her book *The Ethics and Mores of Race* (2011): 'The word "race" is ambiguous, sometimes referring to skin colour, other times to skin colour and group history, sometimes to biology and genealogy, other times to culture by itself or culture combined with other factors.'

In short, there are no sure foundations for biologists to conduct their investigations.

SHOULD WE IDENTIFY RACE?

Given that the biology is suspect, should we just do away with the concept of 'race' altogether? It's scientifically insubstantial and leads to racism – so maybe we should just consign it to the rubbish heap along with those other outdated scientific ideas like phlogiston and Flat Earth.

That's the rationale behind what's known as the 'colour-blindness principle' popular in some liberal circles. This principle states that, whether hiring for a job or searching for a soulmate, 'race' should never be an active ingredient in our decision-making. Racial discrimination should have no part in our public, professional or private lives.

The aim behind the colour-blindness principle may be a worthy one, but there are good reasons to be wary of it. For one thing, while race may be an inert concept in the biological sciences, it's an undeniable part of our social reality. We use it to talk about our own and other people's identities – and while racial categories are 'socially constructed', that doesn't mean they're not real and don't have real consequences for the real people really grouped by them.

Tommie Shelby and Reni Eddo-Lodge

have both shown that it's politically important to have a way of specifying what race is, because we need to identify groups that have been the victims of racial oppression. In her book *Why I'm No Longer Talking to White People About Race* (2017), Eddo-Lodge writes the following:

'My blackness has been politicized against my will, but I don't want it wilfully ignored in an effort to instil some sort of precarious, false harmony.'

Black people have been oppressed because of the socially constructed idea of race. As Eddo-Lodge indicates, her racial identity has been 'politicized' against her will. It's socially active and she has suffered as a result. The thought, then, is that while there's little biological justification for 'race', we shouldn't try to flick the colour-blindness switch. If you say 'I just don't see race', you're wilfully ignoring social facts about someone.

It seems, then, that, irrespective of its biological foundations, we need to keep talking about race. Social race is real and needs to be discussed.

CLUB RULES

We all know what it's like to feel 'out of place'. Whether it's your first day at school, or at your new job, everyone has felt that peculiar and unnerving sensation of *not fitting* in. Conjure it up: you don't know what's going on; you don't know where to stand, or who to talk to or what you're expected to say. And you feel a tension around you – a coolness from other people. They know you don't know how to fit in.

But into what?

Sally Haslanger, a social ontologist (someone who looks at social realities), would encourage us to examine these feelings of out-of-placeness in relation to the background beliefs of the society we find ourselves in. These background beliefs are what Karl Marx called 'ideology'. Michel Foucault called them 'discourse' and Pierre Bourdieu talks of 'habitus'. As Haslanger notes, these terms all capture something of the character of this set of structuring beliefs. Marx, Foucault and Bourdieu are talking about a system of ideas, which manifests in habits and ways of talking (or discoursing) about the world.

Think about it in terms of computing. Ideology is like a computer operating system: Windows 8 or Mac OS X. Every one of us has got specific programs running – specific thoughts and feelings – but they only work if we've got a background operating system in place. Sometimes you try running a program (a thought or an idea) and it's not compatible with the background system (so people look at you funny), but most of the time, the OS is there, allowing you to think your everyday thoughts and live your life.

The operating system downloads automatically – which is to say we're not conscious of learning a specific ideology. It's just there, framing our experience. As such, the beliefs and habits it contains are rarely questioned. The brilliant Bell Hooks gives an example of ideological framing in her essay 'Confronting Class in the Classroom' (1994):

'As silence and obedience to authority were most rewarded, students learned that this was the appropriate demeanour in the classroom. Loudness, anger, emotional outbursts, and even something as seemingly innocent as unrestrained laughter were deemed unacceptable ... It is still necessary for students to assimilate bourgeois values in order to be deemed acceptable.'

Most of us accept that classrooms should be quiet, 'polite' and 'respectful' places. If asked to give a justification, you could say it 'facilitates discussion'. (If everyone spoke over everyone else, you'd never learn!) And yet, you could equally say it's important to show *passion* in the classroom. Learning should be exciting – and students should laugh and shout with enthusiasm! As Hooks points out, it's not inevitable that classrooms are structured in the way that they are. The classroom politesse is a function of – to use another Marxist term – a 'bourgeois' ideology.

Might the same be true of other things in our lives? What about our nine-to-five jobs? Our three meals a day? What have we consciously chosen to do – and what is ideologically driven?

JOIN OUR CLUB!

Certain ideologies can lend certain people advantages over others. In the same way that a computer program like Word might work better on a specific operating system, some people can move more easily in one 'habitus' than another. Not because they know the rules particularly well, but because they're 'privileged' by the system. There are background beliefs that favour some folk over others.

The 20th-century French philosopher and novelist Simone de Beauvoir described this kind of 'privileging' of men over women in her book *The Second Sex* (1949):

'I have already said how hostile the street is ... if [a woman] lights a cigarette in a café, if she goes to the cinema alone, an unpleasant incident can quickly occur; she must inspire respect by the way she dresses and behaves ... "Her wings are clipped."'

Our society is shaped by an ideology that privileges men. We download the rules automatically, picking up directions from the way people treat us and appear in books, TV and advertising.

Let's think about this in more concrete terms. Take Joanna and Will. Joanna is a young woman. Will, her boyfriend, is a slightly older man. In most countries, they're supposed to be *legally* treated as equals. But what about *ideologically*? If what Haslanger says is true (and I think it is), Will tends to enjoy powers that Joanna does not. He's routinely given greater credibility. He's seen as the author of his own actions. He's defined in relation to no one but himself.

This is a societal imbalance we'll want to address. But there's a problem here. As the epistemologist Charles W. Mills points out, our ideological biases are hard to spot because we think of them as natural. Sure, Will might love Joanna, but he'll find it hard to see when and how he's being unfairly empowered – because the ideological biases ruling in his favour are so deeply entrenched in society.

As Mills also points out, it's a lot easier to be ignorant of ideology when you're not suffering from its effects. (If you use computer programs that work well in Windows X, you probably won't think about the operating system's flaws.) So not only is Joanna the victim of this bias, but Will is less likely than she is to be aware of it.

We all know that feeling of being 'out of place'. Unfortunately, some of us experience it a great deal more than others. Mills and Haslanger encourage us to assess where our ideological biases lie and which ones we benefit from. Take a moment. Have a think. Have you ever been harassed in the street? Do your bosses or teachers look like people of your social race? When you fail or succeed, do people attribute it to your gender? When you watch a Hollywood blockbuster, who do you identify with? Ignorance of these things might be bliss, but it's also profoundly unfair.

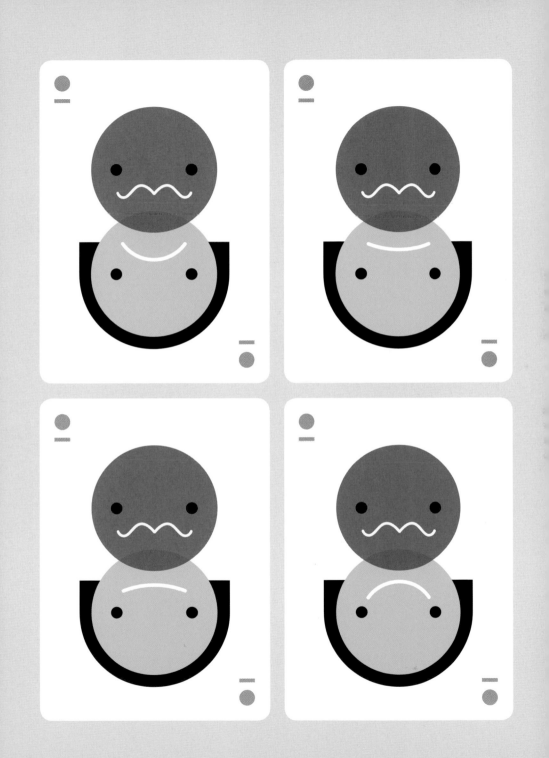

GUILT IS A P
MATTER. RES
IS A POLITIC

ERSONAL
PONSIBILITY
AL ONE.

MAKING AMENDS

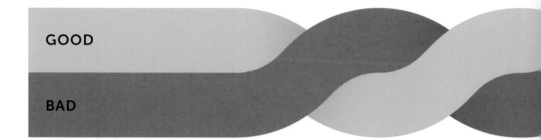

GOOD

BAD

Let's take a clear case of wrongdoing. Bob is a greedy guy and 'morally ambivalent' to boot. He breaks into Hari's house, beats Hari up and steals Hari's money. Bob, it's fair to say, is guilty of this crime. Hari deserves justice, and Bob should be the one to pay. He's 'morally responsible'.

This kind of story fits neatly into our standard model of responsibility. We find an early articulation of this model in Aristotle's *Nicomachean Ethics*, written in the 4th century BC. There, Aristotle states that only certain types of beings can bear responsibility: they must, at the very least, possess the ability to *consciously decide* to do something. You can't, for instance, hold a tree responsible for falling over and crushing

a car; it's not conscious, it didn't *decide* to fall over.

Aristotle elaborates. A conscious agent is only responsible for an act if they've decided to do it freely (they haven't been coerced) and if they know what it is that they're bringing about. Nobody forced Bob to break into Hari's house – he does so freely, out of greed. Nor is he under any illusion about the consequences of his actions. He knows that if he hits Hari, he'll leave bruises, and that the money he takes is not Monopoly money, it's real. So Bob should be held responsible.

This framework of moral responsibility has been serving humans for thousands of years. But things aren't always as simple as Bob's story suggests. There are cases where

responsibility is harder to place. Imagine, for instance, that you're taking a dog out for a walk and it poops – shock! horror! – in a public park. Whose responsibility is it to clean up? And what if your baby scratches a car by flailing with its rattle – who takes responsibility? In neither case do you commit the act, but in both you might reasonably be held responsible.

Let's extend the story. Bob, in addition to being a thief, is a canny investor. After his crime, his business grows. He and his wife enjoy a luxurious lifestyle and have lots of children. A couple of generations down the line, Bob's great-granddaughter, Roberta, starts a family of her own. She's done well out of her great-grandfather's empire – she's

been privately educated, lived in affluent parts of town, and receives top-notch health care. On top of all that, she's a *nice* person. She gives to charity, she's kind to her friends and helps out at a local homeless shelter.

Unfortunately, Bob's crime remains unpunished. Roberta's great-grandfather is long dead, so on the Aristotelian model, the responsible agent can't be held to account. Does this mean *nobody's* responsible? Roberta didn't commit the crime, and might not even know about it. It's not her fault that Harriet, Hari's great-granddaughter, is living a hugely impoverished life because of the unpunished crime suffered by Hari.

How can the Aristotelian account cope with this? It doesn't look like it can.

WHO SHOULD TAKE RESPONSIBILITY?

There are serious forms of injustice which Aristotle's account seems incapable of accommodating. Take, for example, *corporate* responsibility. An oil company sends its ship across the sea, and there's an oil spill. Wildlife is destroyed, water is contaminated. No individual person appears to have acted wrongly. Where does the responsibility lie?

And what about *intergenerational* responsibility? The story of Bob, Roberta, Hari and Harriet might seem contrived, but there are countless examples of historical injustice for which no one (according to Aristotle) can be held responsible.

Consider, for instance, the 'Great' British Empire. It committed innumerable atrocities in the name of queen and country during its centuries-long rule. British society benefitted,

and continues to benefit, from the heinous actions of the colonial regime. The same is true of other European powers, such as France, Holland, Spain, Portugal … (the list, unfortunately, goes on). Yet according to Aristotle, no one can be held responsible since the perpetrators – the agents who committed the crimes – are all long dead.

Then again, maybe the slave-owning Aristotle wasn't the best judge? There are a growing number of philosophers who think he got wrongness all wrong. Here's a short passage from Albert G. Mosley's essay, 'A Defense of Affirmative Action' (1994):

'… human beings are not atomized, self-serving entities. [They] conceive themselves as having distinct family lines and group identities, and are, more often than not,

as concerned with providing benefits to those with whom they identify as they are concerned with benefiting themselves.'

Mosley suggests that Aristotle's individualistic model misses an important dimension of unjust action. We don't always act as self-serving 'atoms'; we act as members of communities. The British colonialists didn't just act for themselves, they acted for their descendants too. The same was true of American slavers – and, in the story above, of Bob.

Mosley's suggestion is in line with the thoughts of the 20th-century political theorist Hannah Arendt. An individual, says Arendt, should take responsibility for other people's actions when those actions were done for the sake of a community with which the individual identifies. Bob committed his crime for the sake of his family. Roberta identifies as a member of that family. As such, she should bear responsibility for her great-grandfather's action.

You might still object. She isn't guilty! She didn't do anything wrong! And in a way, that's right. As Arendt points out in her essay 'Collective Responsibility' (1987), guilt and responsibility are different things. Guilt, she says, is a personal matter. Responsibility is a political one. Roberta might not be guilty but as an issue of political restitution, she can be held responsible as a member of Bob's family and a beneficiary of his unjust deed.

Likewise, citizens might not be guilty of historical, colonial injustices, but we may still be responsible as members of the society that benefits from them.

MORAL RUBBISH

The Earth's a pretty big place, with a circumference at the equator of roughly 25,000 miles (40,000km) and a population of 7.5 billion people. It's not easy to get your head around something so enormous. So let's keep things small to begin with. Let's start with Katy.

Katy's friends are moving to a new flat. They've said she can stay in their old digs for six months – free of charge – while it's being sold. Great! She has a grand old time, living it up in the neighbourhood, spending the rent-money she's saved on partying. She's not very tidy and she lets the plants die, but *hey-ho*! Eventually, the six months are up, and she decides to have a leaving party. Things get rowdy. There's loud music and the neighbours bang on the walls. Katy and her friends spill wine on the sofa and overload the bins – but Katy isn't too fussed. That's the beauty of leaving parties: she's *leaving*!

This, we think, is kind of uncool. For one thing, Katy's actions have harmful effects on her neighbours. She can't hear the sobbing over the rock music, but next door a young couple with toddlers are having a terrible time. There are also the new owners to consider. Temporal neighbours rather than spatial ones – they're going to have to tidy up Katy's mess after she's gone. These are human-centred – or 'anthropocentric' – ethical concerns.

There are also ill effects for nonhumans. The neighbour's dogs, for example, find rock music just as disturbing as their owners do. And remember the plants Katy neglected to water? They may not have been sentient entities, but they were beautiful, rare orchids and now they're shrivelled up and dead.

Take a moment to imagine the uncoolness of Katy's behaviour on a global scale. The consequences of global warming

Rupert Read also talks about anthropocentric concerns but focuses on temporal neighbours – future human generations. Our treatment of the environment is, he says, creating horrible conditions for our descendants. Returning to the themes discussed in Lesson 15, Read says we're committing 'intergenerational injustices'.

There are philosophers who focus on *non-anthropocentric* concerns as well. We've already seen (in Lesson 7) that Peter Singer thinks nonhuman animals are worthy of moral concern. Theorists like Aldo Leopold also believe nonsentient entities, like forests and rivers, are worthy of moral consideration. Remember Katy's orchids? Their death may not constitute an evil for humans, but Leopold thinks there's something intrinsically worrying about killing them. He's concerned that we use and abuse natural entities without fully understanding the complex relations that hold between them (and us).

'A thing is right when it tends to preserve the integrity, stability and beauty of the biotic community. It is wrong if it tends otherwise.'

Anthropocentric or not, the harms caused by human-caused global warming are ethically troubling.

aren't just wilted pot plants and irritated house buyers; the consequences are mass flooding, desertification and death.

Environmental ethicists can be split into two groups. Some focus on *anthropocentric* concerns. William Blackstone, for instance, says that global warming is bad because it's harmful for humans. Obviously so. It's already started to affect people. For instance, islands are being flooded in the Bay of Bengal, and the Tagus River on the Iberian Peninsula, on which millions depend, is drying up.

CAN WE TRUST THE EXPERTS?

There's been a fair amount of philosophical discussion of environmental ethics. Yet most debates you'll hear on the street aren't about whether or not human-caused climate change is harmful – they're about whether or not it's *real*.

I'm not a climate scientist. The description in this chapter of global warming is a basic summary based on what I've learned from the Internet. Climate science, like astrophysics and biochemistry, is a complex field and it takes years to understand its subtleties – so it's inevitable that I'm relying on the evidence of other people when forming opinions about

it. This reliance, however, contains a minor element of epistemic risk. And this is what the 'climate sceptics' focus on. They say: *What if we're trusting the wrong people?*

If you're worried about this, you might benefit from reading the work of the 17th-century French philosopher Blaise Pascal. He is famous for an argument that appears in his *Pensées*, latterly known as 'Pascal's Wager'. The Wager focuses on a hotly debated topic of the day – the existence of God. Is there a supreme deity? In the *Pensées*, Pascal ingeniously shifts the discussion away from evidence *for* or *against* God's existence. He says, instead, that it's better to act as *though* God exists. Why? Because the potential rewards are infinite – an eternity in heaven! And the potential punishments are infinite too – an eternity in hell! These results, being infinite, outweigh any finite rewards (mortal pleasures) or punishments (mortal privations) that you'd enjoy or suffer if God doesn't, in fact, exist.

This principle applies well to the climate sceptic's claim. Maybe human-made climate change isn't real. But it's better to act as if it is. Why? Well, imagine we act as if it's real when it isn't – what are the downsides? We might,

for instance, put up sanctions against oil drilling, fracking or coal mining. In due course, these sanctions will be overturned when they're seen not to be working. That is, they're finite. Imagine, by contrast, that we act as if global warming isn't real, and we're wrong. We'll have depleted finite resources and destroyed millennia-old ecosystems. These are irrevocable, open-ended disasters. The ill-effects for humans are potentially infinite.

There might be a small epistemic risk in trusting climate scientists, but the potential benefits of combatting global warming are *infinite*. These seem like strong betting odds.

TOOLKIT

13

There appears to be no biological justification
for the claim that 'races' are 'natural kinds'.
Nonetheless, it's important to recognize 'race'
as a social category.
Thinking point Are there other 'natural'
groupings – like 'men' and 'women' – that
would also benefit from closer scrutiny?

14

We experience the world through the filter
of ideology and sometimes this encourages
us to give powers to some people rather
than others.
Thinking point Is it possible to find your
ideological biases without the help of others?

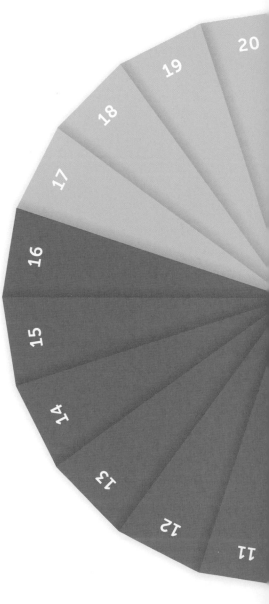

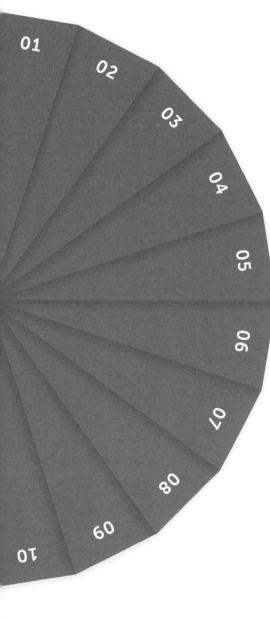

01
02
03
04
05
06
07
08
09
10

15

We often think we're morally responsible only for the actions we've performed ourselves. However, there's a difference between responsibility and guilt. It's possible (and sometimes necessary) to take responsibility for things you haven't done.

Thinking point Can you be guilty of something you haven't done?

16

Global warming results in anthropocentric and non-anthropocentric harms. And even if you're not sure of the scientific evidence for global warming, it's important to act as if you are.

Thinking point Global warming threatens the lives of our descendants – but might the creation of our descendants lead to global warming?

FURTHER LEARNING

READ

The Equality Illusion
Kat Banyard (Faber and Faber, 2011)

The Ethics of Climate Change
James Garvey (Bloomsbury, 2008)

Female Masculinity
Judith Jack Halberstam
(Duke University Press, 1998)

Man Made Language
Dale Spender (Rivers Oram Press, 1980)

LISTEN

**'Reparations' (5 February 2017),
Philosophy Talk**
Ken Taylor and John Perry talk to Michael
Dawson. We're lucky to live in an age of great
philosophical podcasts – Philosophy Talk,
beamed right out of Stanford University, is
one of them!

WATCH

13th
Directed by Ava DuVernay, this brilliant
documentary uncovers the oppressive and
deeply disturbing ideological structure
behind the American prison system.

The Boss of it All (Direktøren for Det Hele)
This Danish comedy directed by Lars von
Trier invites the audience to consider where
responsibility lies (and the lengths people go
to avoid it).

Britain Does Owe Reparations
The renowned Indian politician Shashi
Tharoor talks at the Oxford Union about the
issues of reparation.
www.youtube.com/watch?v=f7CW7S0zxv4

VISIT

Battle of Ideas
Organized by the Institute of Ideas, the Battle
of Ideas festival takes place annually at the
Barbican in London. Topics are wide-ranging,
and tempers often interestingly high.

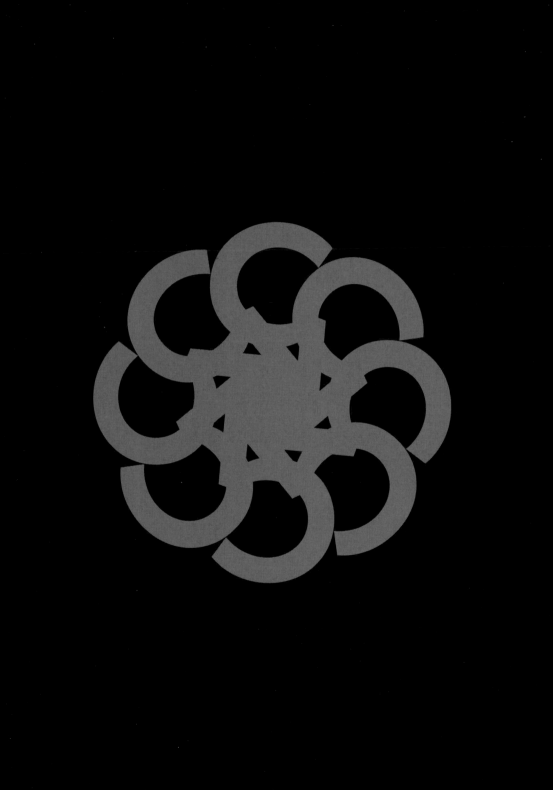

RECREATION

LESSONS

17 HORROR FILMS
Horror movies are scary, right? But the monsters aren't real. How can we be scared of something we know doesn't exist?

18 FINE DINING
Food critics are supposed to have better palates than the rest of us. Does that mean they can tell us what's tasty and what's not?

19 CREATIVE GENIUS
What's creativity? A divine gift? A genetic disposition? A magical power? Do some people have more of it than others – and if so, why?

20 VIRTUAL LIFE
Computer games can be confusing. Sometimes they look more real than real. How worried should we be about this?

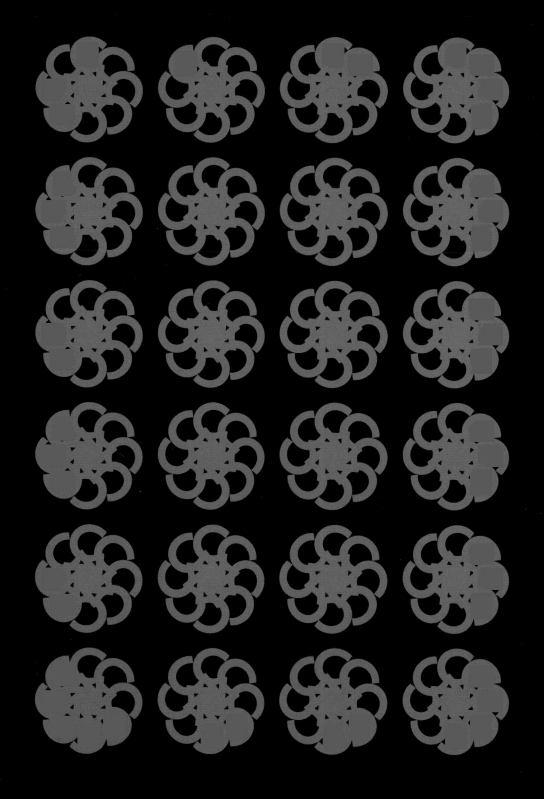

> '**Progessive art can assist people to learn not only about the objective forces at work in the society in which they live, but also about the intensely social character of the interior lives.'**
> *Angela Davis*

Like the sugar from a donut, philosophy covers absolutely everything. That includes donuts. Aesthetics – the study of the nature of beauty – encompasses discussions of taste … and who, really, can discuss taste without discussing donuts? From Plato onwards, philosophers have seen art, literature, hobbies and pastimes as worthy of intellectual attention – so recreation is the focus of our final chapter.

Did *A Nightmare on Elm Street* leave you a gibbering wreck? Did you ever stop to wonder how you can be afraid of something when you know it isn't actually real? In Lesson 17, we'll examine our emotional responses to movie monsters, and the 'paradox of fiction'. It may not stop you screaming during a screening of *The Ring*… but it will help you feel a little better about doing so.

Then again, maybe you don't like to watch horror films. With their B-movie bogeymen and hackneyed tropes, horror films tend to fall within the sphere of what people call 'low art – in contrast to the 'high art' of Mozart or Barbara Hepworth. Does the fact that we rank artworks mean that there's an 'objective standard of taste'?

Our artistic preferences may vary, but one thing most of us agree on is that good art – be it literature, video games or painting – displays creativity. We describe people as 'creative'. That's a good thing for an artist to be, yet it's not immediately obvious what 'creativity' actually is. Thinkers like Plato and Virginia Woolf offer us answers. We'll think creatively about creativity in Lesson 19.

In the final lesson, we'll look at a relatively new art form: computer games. Technology is advancing at an exponential rate and virtual reality (VR) programs are raising serious questions about non-virtual reality (or as it used to be called, 'reality'). How different are our lives from computer simulations – and what does this mean for our sense of identity? As with many of the preceding chapters, we'll examine the idea that our belief in a single, unified self no longer seems as natural as it once it did. Is this okay? Is it preferable? As a single, demonstrably simple self, I leave it to you to decide.

HORROR FILMS

The sweaty palms. The spilled popcorn. The gasps as the monster slithers across the screen. We all know scary movies can be genuinely scary. They can make you tremble and your hair stand on end. They can, quite literally, push you to the edge of your seat. And they're not the only films to provoke emotional reactions. *Spoiler alert*: romantic films can be romantic! They can make your heart skip a beat. And comedies can be funny, thrillers thrilling and dramas dramatic.

That's all fairly uncontroversial. And yet ... if you were *actually* scared by the film monster, wouldn't you burst out of the cinema screaming? Wouldn't you run off to warn your family and friends about the mass-murdering, dream-controlling Freddy Krueger? Surely to be genuinely scared of something, we have to believe there's something to be scared of – but we know Krueger's a figment of Wes Craven's imagination. We know the on-screen action is performed by actors in front of a film crew.

This is what's known as 'the paradox of fiction'. It's a term coined by Colin Radford in his 1975 article, 'How Can We Be Moved by the Fate of Anna Karenina?' His paradox has three premises; all seem true but taken together they appear to contradict one another.

The first premise holds that for us to be emotionally moved by people and circumstances, we need to think they *actually exist* (or existed). This seems plausible, right? We're rarely moved by things we know to be untrue. You might be sad to learn that your pet hamster has died – but it'd make no sense to be sad if you later discovered her alive and well in her hutch.

The second premise holds that when we engage with fiction – books, films, TV and computer games – these 'existence beliefs' are lacking. This seems straightforward too. We don't think Freddy Krueger's real. We know, in fact, that he's made up.

Finally, the third premise states – again, plausibly – that fictional characters and situations actually do move us. We are scared of fictional monsters, we do fall in love with fictional protagonists. *Fiction affects us.*

As Radford points out, it's difficult – nay, impossible – for all these premises to be true. How can we be moved by characters we know don't exist when in order to be moved, we have to believe they exist? *This* is the paradox of fiction.

Philosophers have offered a variety of answers. Eva Schaper, for example, denies the plausibility of premise one: she thinks we're moved, not because we believe some character is really real but because we think they possess certain characteristics worthy of fear or love. Kendall Walton rejects premise three: he thinks we're not genuinely scared — we're just playing a kind of game. We're pretending. Others still question the second premise, suggesting we are sometimes led to suspend our disbelief ... and maybe, not that infrequently, we do suspect that Freddy Krueger is real (and how could we prove otherwise? He hides in your dreams!)

Think about it the next time you go to a scary movie. Are you scared? Or just pretending? Do you sincerely believe the monster is real? And if not ... why are your hands trembling?

Joy

Sadness

USEFUL ... OR DANGEROUS?

Whatever our views about the paradox, the fact is that we are moved by fiction. Some stories make us sad, others make us happy or scared or even angry. Fiction can inspire delicate, subtle emotions. It can imbue us with a sense of justice, or nurture feelings of love towards our partners. This is fiction's power.

And it has more troubling effects as well. Harrowing films can provoke existential angst. Critics of violent fiction often say it contributes to violent attitudes in society (a thought we touched upon in Lesson 12). Quentin Tarantino's films, for instance, have been accused of *glamorizing* violence, and *normalizing* it, such that they encourage people to *be* violent. These putative effects have led people to call for censorship.

There is, however, an ancient thought, found in Aristotle, which stands against the claim that all depictions of violence are damaging. Some, indeed, might be seen to be helpful. Take, for example, one of Tarantino's films, *Inglourious Basterds*. It's graphically violent with gore by the bucketload. It's a revenge fantasy. In it, Tarantino imagines a group of Jewish soldiers blowing up Nazis during the Second World War and – rewriting history – assassinating Adolf Hitler.

The film won't be to everyone's tastes, but it presents a variety of fictional scenarios where historically oppressed people are given the opportunity to redress violent injustices violently. We might think this film nurtures what Aristotle, in his *Poetics*, called 'catharsis'.

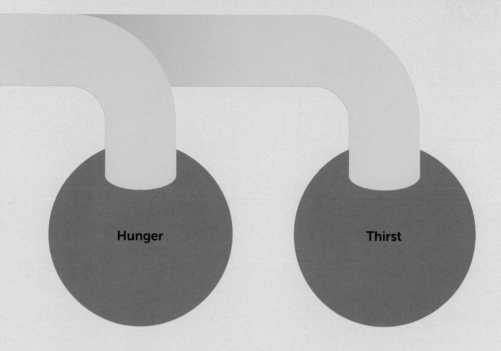

Hunger

Thirst

For Aristotle, emotions are importantly related to morality. For instance, you should cultivate your emotions so that you feel joy when you behave well and sadness when you err. They are bodily motions (hence '*emotions*'), like hunger or thirst, which we should use to motivate us to act in the right way. Some emotional responses are to be nurtured, others avoided – they are to be *controlled* – and among his various methods for controlling them is 'catharsis'. Catharsis is like the releasing of a valve on unhealthy or unhelpful feelings 'A tragedy, then, is the imitation of an action ... with incidents arousing pity and fear, wherewith to accomplish its catharsis of such emotions.'

As he says in the *Poetics*, tragedies arouse pity and fear in such a way that dangerous excesses of these emotions in the audience can be released. The tragedy provokes tears or gasps, and so pity and fear are purged. They're directed towards something fictional, so the audience can focus more clearly on the practical affairs of their daily lives.

Members of groups who have suffered historical injustice may feel anger. But it might be an anger that has no practical target (if, for instance, the perpetrators are dead). Nor might these people want to commit *actual* acts of violence. However, filmic representations of violent retribution might function *cathartically*. They might diffuse the anger, so that the practical, less emotional business of financial reparation can be pursued.

That, at least, would be Aristotle's take. It may be Tarantino's too. But is it yours?

FINE DINING

Are you familiar with Marmite? Vegemite? That black gloopy substance sold in supermarkets? It's a strange, yeasty by-product of the beer-making process ... and people eat it. They willingly ingest it, in all its salty, gooey horror. People love it. Some people (myself included) do not.

Are the Marmite-lovers right when they say that it's delicious? Am I wrong to say it's an abomination? Perhaps you think these questions are ill-fitting. Surely it's just 'a matter of taste'. It's 'subjective'. End of. The same is true for opera and hip-hop and comedies and action movies. Thus, we find in the sphere of aesthetics the Latin dictum: *De gustibus non est disputandum*. Of taste, there can be no dispute!

The 18th-century Scottish philosopher David Hume disputed this. In his famous essay 'Of the Standard of Taste' (1757), he pointed out that while everyone likes different things, there is general agreement that some of these things are better than others.

Most people, for example, would agree that George Eliot's novels have greater artistic worth than John Grisham's. Most will say Frida Kahlo's paintings are more accomplished than those of former American president George W. Bush.

Hume suggests that our collective verdict that Eliot is a better writer than Grisham relies on there being objective standards of taste. There's a measure, outside personal preference, which allows us to say that Kahlo's work is more beautiful than Bush's. But how can we determine this objective standard? Hume's response is that we find the true measure of taste 'in the joint verdict of true judges'. There are some people who are particularly skilled at assessing works of art. Theirs is the opinion we should trust.

This appears to make sense. There *do* seem to be people with better aesthetic senses than others. Wine-tasters, for example, have more developed palates and can detect and articulate subtle ranges of flavours that other people just think of as 'winey'. Similarly, there are connoisseurs of food and theatre.

'Strong sense, united to delicate sentiment, improved by practice, perfected by comparison, and cleared of all prejudice, can alone entitle critics to this valuable character; and the joint verdict of such, wherever they are to be found, is the true standard of taste...'

What Hume means is that a 'true judge' has a refined aesthetic sense and possesses the ability to judge an artwork on its own merits. They have a clearer insight than the rest of us, who lack the training and the disposition, into what makes good art. Sure, they're not infallible – that's why Hume calls for a 'joint verdict' – but together, these judges can lay out the objective standards of taste ... Or so Hume would have us believe.

THE TYRANNY OF TASTE

There's something rather worrying about Hume's claims for aesthetic objectivity.

Consider, again, his grounds for saying there are objective standards. There are works, he says, which have been 'universally found to please in all countries in all ages'. That's a bold claim. Where's his evidence? How extensive is his research? *All* countries in *all* ages? Does this claim even make sense? Take a pretty straightforward example of Western artistic excellence: William Shakespeare's *Hamlet*. How could such a work be made accessible to even a small range of cultures? The audience would have to understand 16th-century English, the social mores (including the fart jokes) and the multi-fold theatrical conventions. How plausible is this? Even if everyone in Europe liked Shakespeare, Hume's claim would still be bad inductive reasoning from too small a sample.

Coupled with this, there are critiques of the politics of Hume's aesthetics. Once we start doubting the objective standards of taste, we're going to start asking what the judges are actually doing. Aestheticians, like Richard Shusterman and Carolyn Korsmeyer, suggest that there's something decidedly sinister about Hume's 'true judges'. Hume is, they say, giving some people the power to say what's beautiful and what's not.

Imagine you go into work one day and the office manager, Alan, confronts you. Alan has an unfortunate fondness for novelty ties. Today he's wearing a really atrocious one with a clown on it. A really creepy clown. Unluckily, people also think of Alan as one of Hume's 'true judges'. As such, he and his fellow judges can now say that novelty ties (particularly ones with clowns on them) are categorically and objectively beautiful and hilarious. It's not just his opinion. It's true. And as a non-judge, it doesn't matter what you think, or how much you hate novelty ties – your tastes are forevermore going to be defined in relation to Alan's standards.

Think about the sorts of people Hume would turn into judges. Think about wine tasters. These are people who have the time and money to taste a heck of a lot of wine to 'refine their palates'. These are people who, as Shusterman puts it, are 'historically socially privileged'. They can swan around at their leisure, swilling alcohol, taking art history courses and reading. This is the subtext of Hume's essay: it's up to people with these privileges to choose what's beautiful.

That, surely, can't be right – can it?

ARE YOU SU
YOU'RE NOT
A COMPUTE
RIGHT NOW?

RE THAT
PLAYING
R GAME

CREATIVE GENIUS

We like it when our artworks, our books, our music and movies are 'creative'. We celebrate the creativity of our authors, composers and games designers. When I say, 'She's so creative,' that's a good thing. But *why*? What is creativity, exactly? What is this peculiar force we value so highly?

There's a tangle of ideas that we associate with the notion of creativity. Originality is one. Obviously, the ability to create is another. But what does it mean to be a creative person? We often characterize a creative act as a type of spasm – we get creative 'bursts of energy', springing seemingly from nowhere and issuing in powerful and original artworks.

This involuntary, spasmodic element appears in the conception of creativity found in Plato's dialogue *Ion*, written in the 5th century BC. There, Plato describes how poets, like Homer and Hesiod, created their works in an unplanned, almost unconscious manner.

They were touched by 'divine inspiration'; they acted, not as conscious agents, but as conduits for some other force. 'Inspiration' comes from the same Latin root as 'respire', and for Plato it was the gods who *breathed* life into the poets' minds.

This idea has persisted, though the 'divine' element has largely disappeared. Creativity in artists has been naturalized (explained in terms of the natural realm rather than the divine). People have creative 'inclinations', 'feelings', 'sentiments' and so on. You might, by a genetic quirk, be a creative person, or prone to bursts of creativity. You might be deathly dull. Creativity is seen to be a character trait, not something that can be taught.

Fun fact: Plato hated poets. In his treatise *The Republic* he had them banished from his ideal city-state (this, despite the poetic verve in his own works). Artists, for Plato, quite literally don't know what they're talking

about. They produce artwork, not from wit or wisdom, but involuntarily. So they shouldn't be celebrated. Nor trusted. In the *Ion*, he has Socrates describe the situation in this way:

'Epic poets who are good at all are never masters of their subject. They are inspired and possessed...'

'Possessed' is a strong word here, particularly for Plato. It implies that the poets lose control of their cognitive faculties. Their fits of creativity are fits of madness – and worst of all, for Plato who prized reason over everything else, they are instances of irrationality. So, out of the Republic they go.

Overreaction? Probably. More recently, philosophers have analyzed the concept of creativity slightly differently. Paisley Livingston thinks that creativity is clearly more than involuntary mental spasming. The following quotation is from his essay 'Poincaré's "Delicate Sieve"' (2009):

'A good artist, it would seem, is not only someone who has the gift of unconsciously generating new combinations ... but someone who has the propensity to react sensitively to his or her own results, selecting those that correspond to a scheme of artistic value.'

In contrast to Plato, Livingston suggests that creativity is more than the unconscious generation of new things. It involves the ability to consider what's being generated and to focus on certain elements rather than others. Not all creativity is wild creativity. It can be *considered*, and ordered in relation to specific frameworks, be they artistic or filmic or literary conventions.

Creative acts need not be irrational at all.

CAN YOU CREATE CREATIVITY?

It's not unusual to hear people being described as 'creative' in the same way they might be described as 'tall' or 'short', or 'cheerful' or 'good at mathematics'. Creativity is included among those traits that people think you have 'naturally'. William Shakespeare, someone might say, was born to be a creative genius.

As we've seen, Plato construed such traits in relation to the gods. These days, we may think some people have a *genetic disposition* to be more creative than others (though, as we saw in Lesson 13, this kind of 'genetic reductionism' can be perilous). Virginia Woolf, the British novelist, took umbrage with this way of thinking. In her work *A Room of One's Own* (1929), she emphasized the extent to which creativity depends on *material circumstance* – and how, as a result, some figures (notably men) have been positioned as more 'creative' than others.

'A woman,' writes Woolf, 'must have money and a room of her own if she is to write fiction.' She gives the example of Judith Shakespeare. Who? Judith, Woolf tells us, is Shakespeare's sister. While Will was off at school, being taught iambic pentameters and metaphor, Judith was stuck at home doing domestic labour. William learns. Judith is chastised for her 'unwomanly' bookish ways. She has chores to do – and so her ability to create, creatively, is restrained, despite her being 'as adventurous, as imaginative, as agog to see the world as he was'.

Woolf causes us to question whether people are born creative or become creative. More importantly, she draws attention to the fact that there are huge differences in who gets to exercise their creativity. Given its power (described in Lesson 17), it's worrying that only certain people have been *allowed* to be creative.

It's a problem. A big one. How do we solve it? Well, for one thing, we should think creatively about how to improve the material conditions of all would-be writers.

VIRTUAL LIFE

Computer games are amazing, aren't they? The graphics on the new PlayStation are so good, they make your eyes hurt. They're higher-definition than reality. The artistry and attention to detail that go into their design are incredible – and the worlds generated in these consoles are breathtaking in their scope and creativity.

Then there's virtual reality technology, like the Oculus Rift headsets that allow you to experience 360-degree immersion in a virtual world. And augmented reality (AR) that supports games like Pokémon GO, mixing gaming with our everyday life, through the prisms of our smartphones.

Yup. Computer games are amazing. And they are well known for provoking powerful philosophical questions.

The 17th-century French philosopher René Descartes is famous for his *Meditations*, in which he nurtures in the reader a radical doubt about the external world. He asks, 'How do I know I'm not dreaming?', and 'How do I know I'm not the victim of some unholy prank by an evil demon?' (I'm paraphrasing). Descartes, of course, wasn't really sceptical about the existence of the external world – and the 'evil demon' hypothesis was used as a method for finding certain truths beyond doubt (like the celebrated thesis, 'I think therefore I am'). Still, these puzzles have stayed with us – and it's easy to see how gaming technology motivates similar ones.

How can you be sure that you're not playing a game right now? A highly naturalistic game that involves sitting and reading a book called *Think Differently?*

In his 2003 paper, 'Are you living in a computer simulation?', the futurologist Nick Bostrom broaches some of these Cartesian worries from an interestingly different perspective. He puts forward what has come to be known as 'The Simulation Argument'.

He starts with two pretty plausible assumptions. First, he proposes that human civilization may one day produce VR technology that renders virtual reality indistinguishable from reality ('technological maturity'). Given the current rate of progress in gaming, this doesn't seem implausible. Second, he thinks virtual worlds, peopled with beings like us, may well become increasingly popular – and again this seems possible, given the demand for games like *The Sims and Second Life*.

With these assumptions in place, he offers us three propositions. One of these, he says, is true.

01. **Almost all civilizations at our stage of technological development will go extinct before they reach technological maturity.**
02. **All technologically mature civilizations will lose interest in creating simulations about human life.**
03. **We are almost certainly living in a computer simulation.**

Bostrom isn't interested in Descartes's 'epistemological' concerns. He doesn't start from a position of doubt. He assumes that everything is exactly as it seems. Computers are getting faster. Technology is blurring the line between what is real and what isn't. His argument is intended to draw out the implications of these advancements by testing one proposal after the other.

Might the first proposition fail to obtain? Yes! Pending nuclear fallout, we might yet achieve technological maturity.

What about proposition two? Looking at our current interests in VR, it seems likely that our enthusiasm for these simulations will continue into the future.

This leaves us with proposition three. Technologically mature civilizations will have the processing power capable of running astronomical numbers of simulations – millions, or billions – so there will be many, many more simulated people like us than non-simulated people.

This leads to the 'simulation hypothesis' that says that it's more likely that we're simulated people than not. Sit with that thought for a moment. How does it make you feel? What implications does it have for you, and the way you live your life?

WHERE IS MY MIND?

For philosophers like Bostrom, there's a distinct possibility we might be very different kinds of beings to the entities we think we are. Maybe we exist in computers, or as brains in vats, or in the mysterious 'cloud'? We would have a very different 'ontological' character. (The Greek *ontos* roughly translates as 'being'.)

We don't, however, have to go quite so far into the realms of science fantasy to question our ontological status. Our online lives, as they exist right now, cause us to question traditional notions of selfhood.

We tend to think of ourselves as humans – as biological beings with discrete physical boundaries. We've got definite limits (our skin). In the normal course of events, our parts don't tend to detach from one another. You think of yourself as a single being that moves around, communicates, has memories, is self-conscious, and has a private inner life.

Donna Haraway and N. Katherine Hayles suggest that recent technological advances encourage us to question this picture. They nurture the thought that we are, perhaps, moving beyond the human ... and becoming 'posthuman'.

In her essay collection, *How We Became Posthuman* (1999), Hayles writes the following:

'In the posthuman, there are no essential differences or absolute demarcations between bodily existence and computer simulation, cybernetic mechanism and biological organism, robot teleology and human goals.'

Is it really the case that the borders between the biological human and computer simulations have dissolved? Perhaps. Where, for instance, do you think your memories are located? There was a time where we would say they're in your head. Social media, however, has changed this. Think about

Facebook timelines. Twitter feeds. These systems collect photos, videos, messages and conversations. They order them. At the click of button I can bring up pictures of my twelfth birthday. And these systems aren't passive repositories of information like photo albums. We're constantly using them. We live through them, communicating with people (some of whom we've never even met, physically). Like the memories in our brains, our online memories are deeply enmeshed in how we interact with each other and construct our identities.

Our memories seem to be spread out across a huge number of online and offline platforms. Perhaps we're not so self-contained as John Locke suggested (in Lesson 9). To echo the question raised by Donna Haraway in her *Cyborg Manifesto* (1984), 'why should our bodies end at the skin?' And if they don't, if we're dispersed, hybridic posthumans, should we be worried?

TOOLKIT

17

The fears we feel when faced with horror films seem to contradict the idea that we can only be scared of things we believe exist. Our emotional responses to fiction might have practical benefits.

Thinking point Is it ever okay to enjoy fictional representations of violence?

18

Hume says there are objective standards of taste that can be identified by 'true judges'. If there aren't such standards, these judges are little more than cultural tyrants.

Thinking point Is it impossible to improve your 'aesthetic sensibilities' if there aren't any objective standards of taste?

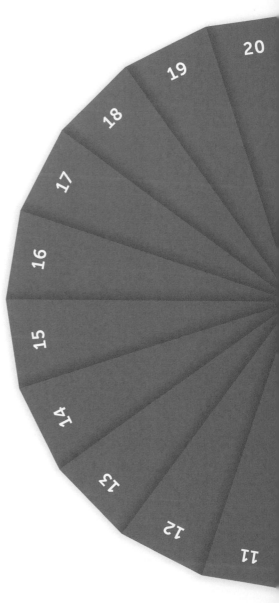

01
02
03
04
05
06
07
08
09
10

19

Whatever creativity actually is, there appears to be a minimum number of material conditions that need to be in place for us to be able to act creatively.
Thinking point If creativity involves the ability to consider consciously and carefully what is being created, can babies be creative?

20

Considerations of technology encourage us to question the kinds of beings that we are. Nick Bostrom suggests we're living in a simulation. Donna Haraway encourages us to think we are spread out across online and off-line platforms.
Thinking point What's so 'real' about 'real life'?

FURTHER LEARNING

READ

Tarantino Unchained
Jelani Cobb, *The New Yorker* (2013)

Hip Hop and Philosophy: Rhyme 2 Reason
Derrick Darby and Tommie Shelby, eds
(Open Court Publishing, 2005)

In Search of Our Mothers' Gardens
Alice Walker (Harcourt, 1983)

Making Sense of Taste: Food and Philosophy
Carolyn Korsmeyer (Cornell
University Press, 1999)

How We Became Posthuman
N. Katherine Hayles (University of
Chicago Press, 1999)

The Cyborg Manifesto
Donna Haraway (Georgetown
University Press, 1984)

LISTEN

'Fiction and the Emotions', Philosophy Bites
With Kathleen Stock and Nigel Warburton.
Philosophy Bites is a great (free!) online
resource of philosophical interviews.

WATCH

Get Out
This breathtaking horror film, directed by
Jordan Peele, is scary, entertaining and a
powerful filmic examination of critical race
theory. A definite must-see.

Inglourious Basterds
It's not to everyone's taste, but Quentin
Tarantino's Second World War revenge
adventure raises interesting questions about
the role of violence in cinema.

VISIT

Brainwash Festival
This annual festival in Amsterdam is one
of the hottest philosophical tickets in the
Netherlands. The event brings together
philosophers and theorists to discuss issues
both old and new – organized in partnership
with the School of Life.

EPILOGUE

That's it – we've reached the end. The Conclusion. Shall we do what people normally do at this point, and conclude? Or is there maybe time for one final thought?

What is a conclusion? It's an opportunity to summarize what's been looked at and learned. It's a chance for an author to complete an argument, and to draw out what follows from their various premises. It's the place where we come to a rest after all the to-ing and fro-ing of the text, the objections and counter-objections and theses and anti-theses. A conclusion is an end-point, a full stop, a final declaration of one's position ... and as such, it's tangibly at odds with the aims of this book, and indeed, of philosophy more generally.

We've looked at a number of interesting, and sometimes bizarre philosophical ideas. They've been confusing to write about – and exciting and irritating and disturbing too – so I can only imagine what they've been like to read. Have they provoked you? Have they made you feel uncomfortable? I hope so. Have you agreed with every single thought on offer? I sincerely hope not. If you're like me, you'll have found yourself oscillating between different opinions, swaying between one position and the next. And that, I think, is part of the point of philosophy. To be continually questioning your position and testing out different perspectives.

It doesn't feel right that a philosophy book should end with a conclusion. Because there's never any problem or puzzle or paradox to which we can't add another question or confusion. Like we said at the start, philosophy isn't really about getting answers, it's about getting puzzled and thinking deeper, and differently. And I hope that's what this book has helped you do.

So let's finish with a lesson learned from the B-movie classics, and write:

The End   ... OR IS IT?

'Philosophy means to be on the way.
Its questions are more essential
than its answers, and every answer
becomes a new question...'
Karl Jaspers

OR DOES IT?

BIBLIOGRAPHY

Kwame Anthony Appiah *Cosmopolitanism: Ethics in a World of Strangers* (Norton, 2006)
Kwame Anthony Appiah 'Liberalism, Individuality, and Identity' (Critical Inquiry, 2001)
Barbara Applebaum *Being White, Being Good* (Lexington Books, 2010)
Hannah Arendt *Eichmann in Jerusalem: A Report on the Banality of Evil* (Viking Press, 1963)
Cathryn Bailey 'We Are What We Eat' (Hypatia, 2007)
Kat Banyard *The Equality Illusion* (Faber and Faber, 2011)
Helen Beebee 'Women and Deviance in Philosophy', in *Women in Philosophy: What Needs to Change* (Oxford University Press, 2013)
David Benatar *Better Never to Have Been* (University Press, 2012)
Marcia Baron *The Moral Status of Loyalty* (Kendall/Hunt, 1984)
Isaiah Berlin 'Two Concepts of Liberty' (Clarendon Press, 1958)
Nick Bostrom 'Are We Living in a Computer Simulation?' (Philosophical Quarterly, 2003)
Pierre Bourdieu *Masculine Domination* (Polity Press, 2001)
Elizabeth Brake *Minimalizing Marriage: Marriage, Morality and the Law* (Oxford University Press, 2012)
Clare Chambers 'The Marriage-Free State', Proceedings of the Aristotelian Society, 134th Session, CXIII(2) (2013)
Jelani Cobb 'Tarantino Unchained' (*The New Yorker*, 2013)
G.A. Cohen *If You're an Egalitarian How Come You're So Rich?* (Harvard University Press, 1996)
Patrisse Cullors and Nyeusi Nguvu 'From Africa to the US to Haiti, Climate Change Is a Race Issue', (*The Guardian*, https://www.theguardian.com/commentisfree/2017/sep/14/africa-us-haiti-climate-change-black-lives-matter)
Derrick Darby and Tommie Shelby *Hip Hop and Philosophy: Rhyme 2 Reason* (Open Court Publishing, 2005)
Stephen Darwall 'Two Kinds of Respect' (Ethics, 1977)
René Descartes *Meditations on First Philosophy* (1641) Accessible via the Gutenberg Project

Lee Edelman *No Future* (Duke University Press, 2004)
Reni Eddo-Lodge *Why I'm No Longer Talking to White People About Race* (Bloomsbury, 2017)
Ian Fraser and Lawrence Wilde *The Marx Dictionary* (Continuum, 2011)
Miranda Fricker *Epistemic Injustice: Power and the Ethics of Knowing* (Oxford University Press, 2007)
James Garvey *The Ethics of Climate Change* (Bloomsbury, 2008)
Graham Greene 'The Virtue of Disloyalty' *The Portable Graham Greene* (Viking, 1973)
Amy Gutmann and Kwame Anthony Appiah *Color Conscious: the Political Morality of Race* (Princeton University Press, 1996)
Judith Jack Halberstam *Female Masculinity* (Duke University Press, 1998)
Donna Haraway *The Cyborg Manifesto* (Georgetown University Press, 1984)
Jenny Harry's letters, in Joseph Green's 'Jenny Harry later Thresher' (*Friends Quarterly Examiner,* 1914)
Sally Haslanger *Resisting Reality: Social Construction and Social Critique* (Oxford University Press, 2012)
N. Katherine Hayles 'Toward Embodied Virtuality' in *How We Became Posthuman* (University of Chicago Press, 1999)
Nancy Holmstrom 'Exploitation' (Canadian Journal of Philosophy, 1977)
bell hooks, 'Class in the classroom', in *Teaching to Transgress* (Routledge, 1994)
David Hume 'Of the Standard of Taste' (1757) Accessible via the Gutenberg project.
Susan James 'Feminism in Philosophy of Mind: the Question of Personal Identity', in *The Cambridge Companion to Feminism in Philosophy* (2000)
Immanuel Kant *Grounding for the Metaphysics of Morals* (1785)
Martin Luther King Jr. 'Loving Your Enemies', (Sermon, 1957) http://kingencyclopedia.stanford.edu/encyclopedia/documentsentry/doc_loving_your_enemies.1.html
Christine Korsgaard 'The Right to Lie: Kant on Dealing with Evil' (*Philosophy and Public Affairs,* 1986)

Carolyn Korsmeyer 'Making Sense of Taste: Food and Philosophy' (Cornell University Press, 1999)

Rae Langton 'Duty and Desolation' in Sexual Solipsism (MIT Press, 2009)

Aldo Leopold For the Health of the Land (Island Press, 2002)

Richard Lewontin The Concept of Race on UCTV.TV (2004)

Paisley Livingston 'Poincaré's "Delicate Sieve": On Creativity and Constraints in the Arts' in The Idea of Creativity (Brill Publishing, 2009)

John Locke Essay Concerning Human Understanding (1689)

Nyanatiloka Mahathera Buddhist Dictionary (Buddhist Publication Soceity, 1972)

Ruth Barcan Marcus Moral Dilemmas and Consistency The Journal of Philosophy 77(3) (1980)

Charles Mills The Racial Contract (Cornell University Press, 1997)

Albert Mosley 'A Defense of Affirmative Action' in Contemporary Debates in Applied Ethics, (Blackwell Publishing, 2005)

Robert Murray Unknown White Male (Shooting People Films, 2005)

Martha Nussbaum The Therapy of Desire (Princeton University Press, 1994)

Susan Okin 'Mistresses of Their Own Destiny: Group Rights, Gender, and Realistic Rights of Exit' (Ethics, 2002)

Onora O'Neill 'Demandingness and Judgment' (2007)

Judith Orr Marxism and Women's Liberation (Bookmarks, 2015)

Blaise Pascal Pensées (1670) (accessible on project Gutenberg)

Jennifer Pitts A Turn to Empire: The Rise of Imperial Liberalism in Britain and France (Princeton University Press, 2005)

Plato Ion (380 BCE). Accessible on the Internet Classic Archive

Michael Puett and Catherine Gross-Loh The Path (Simon & Schuster, 2016)

Colin Radford 'How Can We Be Moved by the Fate of Anna Karenina?' (Proceedings of the Aristotelian Society, 1975)

Phyllis Rooney 'Philosophy, adversarial argumentation, and embattled reason' (Informal Logic, 2010)

Amelie Rorty 'Relativism, Persons, and Practices' in Relativism: A Contemporary Anthology (Columbia University Press, 2010)

Tina Rulli 'The Ethics of Procreation and Adoption' (Philosophy Compass 11/6, 2016)

Tommie Shelby We Who Are Dark (Harvard University Press, 2005)

Sydney Shoemaker Self-Knowledge and Self-Identity (1963)

Richard Shusterman 'The Scandal of Taste' (The Philosophical Forum, 1989)

Richard Sorabji Emotion and Peace of Mind (Oxford University Press, 2000)

Dale Spender Man Made Language (Rivers Oram Press, 1980)

Charles Taylor 'Explanation and Practical Reason' in Philosophical Arguments (Harvard University Press, 1995)

Shashi Tharoor, 'Britain Does Owe Reparations' (2015) https://www.youtube.com/watch?v=f7CW/S0zxv4

Mark Twain (Samuel Clemens), 'On Loyalty', Notebook (Harper, 1935)

Alice Walker In Search of Our Mother's Gardens (Harcourt, 1983)

Virginia Woolf A Room of One's Own (Penguin, 1929)

Fiona Woollard (2016) 'Mother Knows Best: Pregnancy, Applied Ethics and Epistemically Transformative Experiences', http://fionawoollard.weebly.com/mother-knows-best.html

Naomi Zack The Ethics and Mores of Race (Rowman and Littlefield, 2011)

At BUILD+BECOME we believe in building knowledge that helps you navigate your world.

Our books help you make sense of the changing world around you by taking you from concept to real-life application through 20 accessible lessons designed to make you think. Create your library of knowledge.

**BUILD +
BECOME**

www.buildbecome.com
buildbecome@quarto.com

@buildbecome
@QuartoExplores

Through a series of 20 practical and effective exercises, all using a unique visual approach, Michael Atavar challenges you to open your mind, shift your perspective and ignite your creativity. Whatever your passion, craft or aims, this book will expertly guide you from bright idea, through the tricky stages of development, to making your concepts a reality.

We often treat creativity as if it was something separate from us – in fact it is, as this book demonstrates, incredibly simple: creativity is nothing other than the very core of 'you'.

Michael Atavar is an artist and author. He has written four books on creativity – *How to Be an Artist, 12 Rules of Creativity, Everyone Is Creative* and *How to Have Creative Ideas in 24 Steps – Better Magic*. He also designed (with Miles Hanson) a set of creative cards *'210CARDS'*.

He works 1-2-1, runs workshops and gives talks about the impact of creativity on individuals and organisations. www.creativepractice.com

MICHAEL ATAVAR

BUILD+ BECOME

BEING CREATIVE

BE INSPIRED. UNLOCK YOUR ORIGINALITY.

CREATIVITY BEGINS WITH YOU.

Using a unique, visual approach to explore the science of behaviour, *Read People* shows how understanding why people act in certain ways will make you more adept at communicating, more persuasive and a better judge of the motivations of others.

The increasing speed of communication in the modern world makes it more important than ever to understand the subtle behaviours behind everyday interactions. In 20 dip-in lessons, Rita Carter translates the signs that reveal a person's true feelings and intentions and exposes how these signals drive relationships, crowds and even society's behaviour. Learn the influencing tools used by leaders and recognise the fundamental patterns of behaviour that shape how we act and how we communicate.

Rita Carter is an award-winning medical and science writer, lecturer and broadcaster who specialises in the human brain: what it does, how it does it, and why. She is the author of *Mind Mapping* and has hosted a series of science lectures for public audience. Rita lives in the UK.

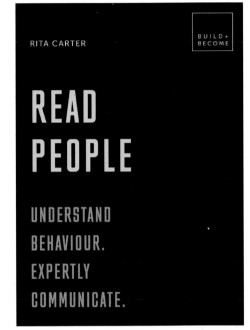

RITA CARTER

BUILD + BECOME

READ PEOPLE

UNDERSTAND BEHAVIOUR. EXPERTLY COMMUNICATE.

CAN YOU SPOT A LIE?

CATHERINE BLYTH

BUILD+
BECOME

ENJOY TIME

STOP RUSHING.

BE MORE PRODUCTIVE.

October 2018

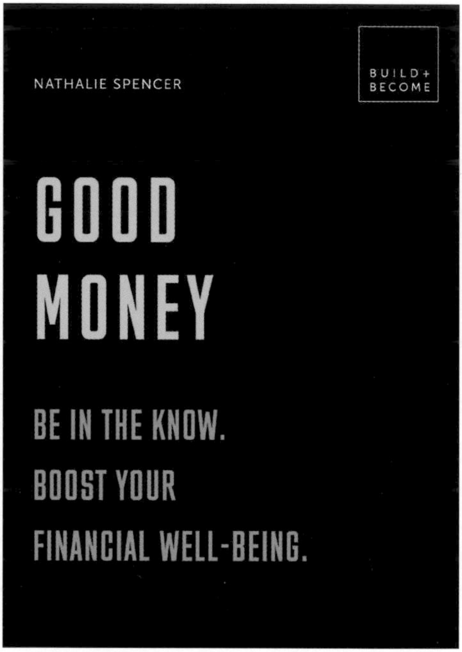

NATHALIE SPENCER

BUILD+
BECOME

GOOD MONEY

BE IN THE KNOW.

BOOST YOUR

FINANCIAL WELL-BEING.

October 2018

Using a unique, visual approach, Gerald Lynch explains the most important tech developments of the modern world – examining their impact on society and how, ultimately, we can use technology to achieve our full potential.

From the driverless transport systems hitting our roads to the nanobots and artificial intelligence pushing human capabilities to their limits, in 20 dip-in lessons this book introduces the most exciting and important technological concepts of our age, helping you to better understand the world around you today, tomorrow and in the decades to come.

Gerald Lynch is a technology and science journalist, and is currently Senior Editor of technology website TechRadar. Previously Editor of websites Gizmodo UK and Tech Digest, he has also written for publications such as *Kotaku* and *Lifehacker*, and is a regular technology pundit for the BBC. Gerald was on the judging panel for the James Dyson Award. He lives with his wife in London.

GERALD LYNCH

BUILD + BECOME

GET TECHNOLOGY

BE IN THE KNOW.
UPGRADE YOUR FUTURE.

KNOW TECHNOLOGY TODAY, TO EQUIP YOURSELF FOR TOMORROW.

NANOROBOTS

In the 1966 film *Fantastic Voyage*, the members of a submarine crew shrink down to a microscopic size and are inserted into the body of a sick man, in the hope that they'll be able to repair damage to his brain from the inside. Half a century later, we've not quite perfected the shrink ray, but the concept of using tiny technologies inside the body to improve health and aid recovery in sickness and injury is one that's increasingly explored – and actively developed.

Nanotechnology, and the associated robotics field of nanorobotics, looks at the ways technology can be used to influence change on matter at the nanoscale. To give some sense of perspective, a nanometre is a measurement of one billionth of a metre, or 10^{-9}m. A strand of hair is 100,000 nanometres wide, while a water molecule would measure less than a single nanometre across. So nanotechnology is looking to work accurately within a fine scale far beyond what standard microscopes can see – at a level where the very building blocks of life are at play.

There's no one defining form of nanotechnology, nor is there one leading use but there are immediate benefits to developing nanorobotics for healthcare. If you can manipulate molecules at such a granular level, or even at a slightly larger scale, you can more easily treat and cure the root causes of diseases.

Take the concept of a nanorobot designed to work within a blood vessel. Though it may lack the *Fantastic Voyage*'s human crew, the film's submarine-like craft makes for a surprisingly good model for how a nanorobot could be shaped. Like a tiny torpedo, a nanorobot could travel along a blood vessel, equipped with a miniature payload of medicine or tiny tools to perform surgery with unparalleled accuracy.

Inserted into a patient inside a biodegradable pill or through a simple injection, the nanorobot could propel itself around the waterways of the circulatory system with some kind of mechanical tail, like the flagellum that allow bacteria to move around the body. Or, the robot could use a patient's own blood to move forward, generating a magnetic field to draw in conductive liquids, forcing them out through a pump and creating thrust like a water pistol.

70

A nanometre is a measurement of one-billionth of a metre.

A strand of hair is 100,000 nanometres wide.

DNA is 2.5 nanometres wide and a water molecule is 0.275 nanometres wide

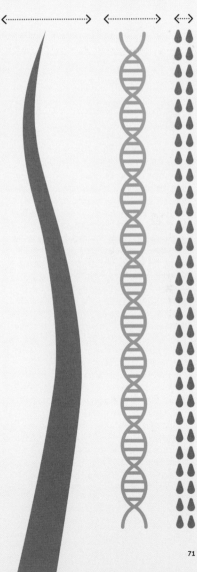

It's a great challenge finding a fuel source that's safe to use within the human body, and one that can provide enough energy to carry out the task at hand within such a small enclosure.

Nuclear power systems have been considered and dismissed, given the danger that radiation poses to human cell structure. You could link the nanorobot to an external power source, but that limits its manoeuvrability, and increases the potential for internal damage to the patient. An interesting alternative is to use the human body itself as a power source, either by inducing a chemical reaction between the nanobot and a patient's blood to create fuel, or by fitting the nanobot with electrodes that could interact with electrolytes found naturally in blood to create a miniature onboard battery.

09
BUILD +
BECOME

SHRINKING THE SURGEON

As you can tell from the previous scenario alone, the challenges faced by engineers in nanorobotics are great, but the potential benefit to come from solving these problems is even more astounding.

Take a cancer sufferer, for instance. Depending on the form of cancer that a patient is fighting, they may currently have to contend with deeply invasive, painful surgery and a debilitating treatment programme. Both take a great physical and emotional toll on the body. A nanobot could work within the body to cut away cancerous tissue with minute accuracy, while delivering the drugs given in a chemotherapy session direct to the source, rather than relying on the circulatory system to eventually bring them to their intended target. This has the potential to cut down the required dosage and length of a course of chemotherapy treatment considerably.

As western diets become increasingly decadent, the healthcare profession increasingly has to deal with problems created by arterial plaque too. Fats like cholesterol build up within artery walls, causing the space within which blood travels through the body to narrow. A tiny nanobot could work like a tunnel-boring machine within an artery, carefully cleaning away the fatty build-up. These procedures, rather than requiring a hospital stay, could even become

outpatient treatments: you could receive a prescription from a doctor and pick up a course of pre-programmed nanobots from your chemist, ready to be taken with a glass of water before meals.

All this is before considering the potential for nanobots to work together. A 'swarm' of nanobots could be deployed to carry out several tasks at once, networked together to achieve something that a single nanobot could not, perhaps taking on protozoa or even relatively large worms.

But why stop there? The futurist Ray Kurzweil envisions a future in which we live with nanobots inside our bodies 24 hours a day, 365 days a year, working alongside our brains to make sure we're forever at our funniest, smartest and most productive. Connecting wirelessly to cloud computing services, they could allow us to interface with the internet – and other humans – remotely at will, with just a thought. While his prediction sees this revolution beginning somewhat dubiously within the next two decades, it's easy to see this as the ultimate goal of nanorobotics.

72

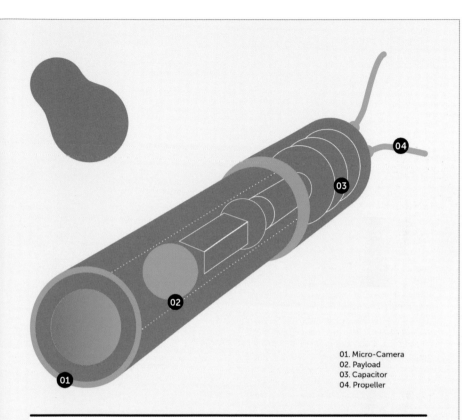

01. Micro-Camera
02. Payload
03. Capacitor
04. Propeller

Every single cell in your body contains a copy of your genetic code, known as your genome. It changes across generations, passed down by your parents, and is made up of DNA, defining your traits and characteristics, from your athleticism to your intelligence. With the entire human genome now sequenced and deciphered, we've been able to use it to help identify some of the undesirable traits too – the mutations that cause diseases.

CRISPR-Cas9 is a tool that lets us edit these sections of our DNA. It's a pair of molecules created and used by scientists to hunt down unwanted parts of DNA and cut them out, either leaving the body to then heal itself, or inserting a desired replacement DNA strand instead. Do this to reproductive or embryonic cells, and the changes are permanently passed down, creating a new inherited code.

These gene-editing techniques could be instrumental in curing hereditary diseases such as cystic fibrosis. However, they also have more controversial uses – could (and should) we be able to use these tools to create 'designer babies', or to tweak the DNA of creatures harmful to humans, wiping out entire species like malaria-carrying mosquitoes?

73

ACKNOWLEDGEMENTS

Every writing venture is a collaborative enterprise – and this one is no different. This book is the product of numerous conversations, with the philosophers included in these pages, and many other people besides. My editor, Lucy Warburton, has been constantly on hand with encouragement and editing prowess – and Victoria Marshallsay has done some sterling copy editing and proofreading. Nathaniel Adam Tobias ~~Coleman~~ has been a source of intellectual inspiration. The wonderful readers include Elianna Fetterolf, Jonathan Nassim, Joanna Burch-Brown, Thomas Quinn, Senuthuran Bhuvanendra and Chris Meyns. Anna, Seb, Axa and the Platform gang helped me test these ideas out. James Garvey and Liza Thompson have kept my spirits up, Harriet and David have kept them confused, and Emily, Viv, Mya, Flo and Luke have done an able job of soothing them. I owe further debts to temporally-and-spatially extended family members and friends. Most of all, Esther McManus has informed me (and by extension, this book), with her wisdom and her wit. I can say with confidence that the errors are all my own.

Adam Ferner has worked in academic philosophy both in France and the UK – but it's philosophy *outside* the academy that he enjoys the most. In addition to his scholarly research, he writes regularly for *The Philosophers' Magazine,* works at the Royal Institute of Philosophy and teaches in schools and youth centres in London.